From the publisher of
Successful Farming® Magazine

Busy Woman's Slow Cooker
cookbook
Meals Ready and Waiting!

by Linda Burgett

D1308111

Better Homes and Gardens®
Test Kitchen

Including favorite recipes from the
Better Homes and Gardens® Test Kitchen

This seal assures
you that the recipe
has been tested in
the Better Homes
and Gardens®
Test Kitchen. This
means the recipe
is practical and
reliable, and meets
our high standards
for great taste.

Busy Woman's
Slow Cooker Cookbook

Author: Linda Burgett

Art Director: Kathy Grove

Project Marketing Manager: Diana Willits

Marketing Associate: Brenda Torsky

Successful Farming® Magazine

Publisher: Scott Mortimer

Editor In Chief: Loren Kruse

Vice President/Group Publisher: Tom Davis

Busy Woman's Slow Cooker Cookbook
(ISBN 978-069630013-4) is published by
Successful Farming® magazine,
Meredith Corporation, 1716 Locust Street,
Des Moines, IA 50309-3023.

www.successfulfarmingbooks.com

Con Queso Dip, *page 18*

Busy Woman's Slow Cooker Cookbook

Beef Stew, *page 66*

Fixin Beef Burgers, *page 155*

Creamy Garlic Chicken, *page 219*

Linda Burgett
Author

From My Kitchen To Yours

How do you have a home cooked meal ready at dinner time when you have to be at work or school all day? How can you have delicious dishes ready to eat after shopping, an afternoon at the movies, or after church?

Turn to your trusted slow cooker or Crock Pot. A few minutes of preparation, turn it on, then come home and enjoy. Fix it, do what you have to do, or want to do, then enjoy good homemade food.

We are sure you will enjoy the ease of using BUSY WOMAN'S SLOW COOKER COOKBOOK and making and eating the great food.

Mocha Coffee, page 6

Taco Cheese Dip, page 18

BEVERAGES, DIPS, AND APPETIZERS

WIDE AWAKE COFFEE

    3 cups half-and-half
    3/4 cup maple syrup
    3 cups strong coffee

In slow cooker, combine all ingredients. Cover. Cook on high 1 or 1½ hours. Makes 6 servings.

MOCHA COFFEE

    1 cup instant cocoa mix
    ½ cup instant coffee crystals
    8 cups hot water
    Whipped topping

In slow cooker, combine all ingredients except whipped topping. Mix well. Cook on high 1 or 1½ hours. Mix and reduce heat to low. Cover. Cook until hot. Serve with whipped topping. Makes 8 servings.

MOCHA CAPPUCCINO

- 6 cups hot strong coffee
- 3/4 cup half-and-half
- 6 tablespoons chocolate syrup
- 7 teaspoons sugar

In slow cooker, combine all ingredients. Cook on high 1 or 1½ hours. Makes 6 servings.

HOT IRISH MOCHA

- 6 cups hot strong brewed coffee
- 4 (1.25 ounce) envelopes Irish cream instant cocoa mix
- 2 cups half-and-half

In slow cooker, combine all ingredients. Mix well. Cook on high 1 to 1½ hours or until very hot. Note: great for a brunch. Makes 8 servings.

HOT PARTY PUNCH

     1 quart cranberry juice
     1 cup orange juice
 1½ cups sugar
     ¼ cup lemon juice
     2 quarts hot water
     ¼ cup red cinnamon candies

In slow cooker, combine all ingredients. Mix until
sugar has dissolved. Cover. Cook on high 1½ to 2
hours. Makes 12 to 15 servings.

HOT JUICE WARM-UPS

     1 cup pineapple juice
 1½ cups cranberry juice
 1½ cups hot water
     3 cups orange juice
 1½ teaspoons lemon juice

In slow cooker, combine all ingredients. Cover.
Cook on low 1 to 1½ hours. Makes 6 servings.

CARAMEL APPLE CIDER

- 1 gallon apple cider
- 6 cinnamon sticks
- 1 (10 ounce) jar caramel ice cream topping
- 1 (14 ounce) can whipped cream

In slow cooker, combine cider and cinnamon sticks. Cover. Cook on low 2 to 4 hours. Pour into mugs. Top each with 1 teaspoon caramel topping and whipped cream. Drizzle additional caramel topping over whipped cream. Makes 15 servings.

SPICY HOT CIDER

- 8 cups apple cider
- 1 cup red cinnamon candies

In slow cooker, combine all ingredients. Mix well. Cover. Cook on high 1½ hours or until candies are melted. Makes 8 servings.

HOT CRAN-APPLE CIDER

6 cups apple cider
2 cups cranberry juice
1 (4 inch) cinnamon stick

In slow cooker, combine all ingredients. Mix well.
Cook on high 1½ to 2 hours. Makes 8 servings.

HOT CIDER PUNCH

2 quarts apple cider
1 cup orange juice
1 cup pineapple juice
4 cinnamon sticks

In slow cooker, combine all ingredients. Cover.
Cook on low 2 to 4 hours before serving.

SIPPIN APPLE CIDER

1	gallon apple cider
2	cups sugar
3	cups orange juice
1/2	cup lemon juice

In slow cooker, combine apple cider and sugar. Mix well. Cook on high 1 1/2 hours. Add orange juice and lemon juice. Mix well. Cover. Cook an additional 1 hour. Makes 15 to 18 servings.

CHILL OUT APPLE JUICE

8	cups apple juice
1	(10 ounce) package sweet frozen sliced strawberries
1/2	teaspoon whole cloves

In slow cooker, combine all ingredients. Mix well. Cover. Cook on low 2 1/2 to 3 hours. Makes 8 servings.

MAD ABOUT MUSHROOMS

1 (1 ounce) package beefy mushroom soup mix
1/4 cup sour cream
1/4 cup half-and-half
2 pounds button mushrooms

In slow cooker, combine soup mix, sour cream, and half-and-half. Add mushrooms. Mix well. Cover. Cook on low 2 to 3 hours.

EASY ARTICHOKE DIP

1 (14 ounce) can artichoke hearts, drained, chopped
1 (8 ounce) container sour cream
1 (1 ounce) package dry onion soup mix
1 cup shredded mozzarella cheese
1 cup mayonnaise

In slow cooker, combine all ingredients. Cover. Cook on low 2 to 3 hours.

ARTICHOKE DIP

- 2 cups frozen spinach, cooked, drained, chopped
- 1 (14 ounce) can artichoke hearts, drained, chopped
- 1/2 cup mayonnaise
- 1/2 cup Alfredo sauce
- 3/4 teaspoon garlic salt
- 1 cup shredded Swiss cheese

In slow cooker, combine all ingredients. Mix well. Cover. Cook on low 2 to 3 hours. Serve with tortilla chips, vegetables, or bread.

DON'T BE A CRAB DIP

- 1 pound Velveeta® cheese, cubed
- 1 stick butter or margarine, cubed
- 2 (6 ounce) cans crabmeat, drained

In slow cooker, combine all ingredients. Cover. Cook on low 2 to 3 hours.

SEASIDE CLAM DIP

2	pints clams, rinsed, drained
2	(8 ounce) packages cream cheese
1	cup sour cream
1/3	cup creamy horseradish

In slow cooker, combine all ingredients. Mix well.
Cover. Cook on low 2 to 3 hours. Serve with chips.
Makes 8 to 10 servings.

CHEESY CRAB DIP

1 pound Velveeta® cheese, cubed
2 (8 ounce) packages cream cheese
2 (6 ounce) cans crabmeat, drained

In slow cooker, combine all ingredients. Mix well.
Cover. Cook on low 1½ to 2 hours. Serve with
crackers.

CHEESE & SHRIMP DIP

2 (8 ounce) packages cream cheese
2 (10¾ ounce) cans cheddar cheese soup
2 (4½ ounce) cans shrimp, drained
¼ cup diced green onion

In slow cooker, add cream cheese. Cover. Cook
on low until cheese melts. Add remaining
ingredients. Mix well. Cover. Cook 1½ to
2 hours. Makes 8 to 12 servings.

PARTY TIME SHRIMP DIP

1 (10¾ ounce) can cream of shrimp soup
1 (8 ounce) package cream cheese, softened
¼ cup finely chopped green bell pepper
2 tablespoons finely chopped onion

In slow cooker, combine all ingredients. Mix well. Cover. Cook on low 2 to 3 hours. Stir after 1 hour of cooking. Makes 2⅓ cups.

TACO DIP

2 cups shredded cheddar cheese
2 (16 ounce) cans refried beans
1 (2¼ ounce) can chopped black olives
1 (1 ounce) package taco seasoning mix

In slow cooker, combine all ingredients. Mix well. Cover. Cook on low 3 to 4 hours. Serve with tortilla chips.

TACO CHEESE DIP

2 pounds Velveeta® cheese, cubed
2 (10 ounce) cans diced tomatoes with
   green chiles
2 teaspoons taco seasoning

In slow cooker, combine all ingredients. Cover.
Cook on low 2½ to 3 hours. Stir after 1 hour and
before serving. Serve with tortilla chips. Makes
6 to 8 servings.

CON QUESO DIP

1 (14½ ounce) can chopped tomatoes
1 (4 ounce) can chopped green chiles
½ cup diced onion
2 cups shredded Monterey Jack cheese

In slow cooker, combine all ingredients. Mix well.
Cover. Cook on low 2 to 3 hours or high 1½ hours.
Serve with tortilla chips. Makes 6 to 8 servings.

CHILE CON QUESO DIP

2 (15 ounce) cans chili without beans
1/3 cup diced onion
1 (16 ounce) jar hot picante sauce
1 (8 ounce) package shredded cheddar cheese

In slow cooker, combine all ingredients. Cover. Cook on low 2½ to 3 hours. Serve with chips. Makes 6 to 10 servings.

SALSA MEXI DIP

2 (16 ounce) cans refried beans
2 cups shredded cheddar cheese
1 cup salsa
1 cup chopped green chiles

In slow cooker, combine all ingredients. Mix well. Cover. Cook on low 2 to 3 hours. Serve with tortilla chips. Makes 2 cups.

NACHO PARTY SNACK DIP

- 2 (16 ounce) packages shredded cheddar cheese
- ½ cup chopped green chiles
- ⅓ cup diced onion
- ½ teaspoon chili powder
- 1 cup diced tomatoes

Coat inside slow cooker with nonstick cooking spray. In slow cooker, combine all ingredients. Mix well. Cover. Cook on high 1½ hours. Mix well. Cover. Cook on low until hot and cheese has melted.

GAME TIME CHEESE DIP

- 2 pounds ground beef, browned, drained
- ½ cup diced onion
- 1 (16 ounce) jar cheese spread
- 1 (8 ounce) jar salsa

In slow cooker, combine all ingredients. Mix well. Cover. Cook on low 3 to 4 hours. Serve with tortilla chips. Makes 8 to 10 servings.

TIPSY CHEESE DIP

2 (8 ounce) packages Mexican cheese
1 cup thick and chunky salsa
1/2 cup beer

In slow cooker, combine all ingredients. Mix well.
Cover. Cook on low 2 to 3 hours. Serve with
tortilla chips. Makes 2 1/2 cups.

SIZZLIN BEEF DIP

1 1/2 pounds lean ground beef, browned, drained
1 (15 ounce) can chili without beans
8 ounces Mexican-style Velveeta®
cheese, cubed
1/2 cup chopped green chiles

In slow cooker, combine all ingredients. Mix well.
Cover. Cook on low 2 1/2 to 3 hours. Makes 6 to 8
servings.

PEPPERONI DIP

2 (14 ounce) jars pizza sauce
2 (10 ounce) packages pepperoni slices, diced
1/2 cup grated Parmesan cheese
1 cup shredded mozzarella cheese

In slow cooker, combine all ingredients. Mix well. Cover. Cook on low 2 to 3 hours. Serve with crackers or bread sticks. Makes 8 to 10 servings.

ITALIAN PIZZA DIP

1 pound Italian sausage, browned, drained
1/3 cup chopped onion
1/3 cup sliced pepperoni, chopped
2 (14 ounce) jars pizza sauce
1 cup shredded mozzarella cheese

In slow cooker, combine all ingredients. Mix well. Cover. Cook on low 3 to 4 hours. Serve with bread sticks or crackers. Makes 8 to 10 servings.

PIZZA DIP

> 1 pound ground beef
> 2 (14 ounce) jars pizza sauce
> 1 (16 ounce) package shredded mozzarella cheese

In slow cooker, combine all ingredients. Mix well. Cover. Cook on low 3 to 4 hours. Serve with bread sticks or crackers. Makes 8 to 10 servings.

HAM & CHEESE DIP

> 1 (8 ounce) package cream cheese, softened
> 1 cup sour cream
> 2 (2½ ounce) packages ham, diced
> 2 green onions, diced

In slow cooker, combine all ingredients. Cover. Cook on low 2 to 3 hours. Serve with bagel chips, tortilla chips, or crackers.

HAM & VEGGIE DIP

- 2 (4 ounce) packages vegetable cream cheese, softened
- 1 cup sour cream
- 1 teaspoon garlic powder
- 2 (2½ ounce) packages ham, diced
- 2 green onions, diced

In slow cooker, combine cream cheese, sour cream, and garlic powder. Mix until smooth. Add ham and onion. Mix well. Cover. Cook on low 2 to 3 hours. Serve with bagel chips, mini bagels, or crackers.

ONION DIP

- 3 (8 ounce) packages cream cheese, softened
- 2 cups grated Parmesan cheese
- 1 onion, finely chopped
- ½ cup mayonnaise

In slow cooker, combine all ingredients. Mix well. Cover. Cook on low 2 to 3 hours. Serve with crackers or chips.

C'MON OVER CHEESE DIP

3 (15 ounce) cans chili
½ cup diced onion
2 (8 ounce) packages cream cheese
2½ cups shredded cheddar cheese

In slow cooker, combine all ingredients. Mix well.
Cover. Cook on low 3 to 4 hours. Serve with
tortilla chips. Makes 10 to 12 servings.

EASY PARTY CHEESE DIP

- 2 pounds Velveeta® cheese, cubed
- 2 cups salsa
- ½ cup diced onion
- 2 cups sour cream

In slow cooker, combine all ingredients. Mix well. Cover. Cook on low 2½ to 3 hours. Makes 12 to 15 servings.

BROCCOLI CHEESE DIP

- 2 (10 ounce) packages frozen chopped broccoli, thawed
- 2 (10¾ ounce) cans cream of mushroom soup
- ¼ cup sour cream
- 8 ounces Mexican-style Velveeta® cheese, cubed
- 8 ounces Velveeta® cheese, cubed
- 1½ teaspoons garlic salt

In slow cooker, combine all ingredients. Mix well. Cover. Cook on low 2 to 3 hours.

BROCCOLI DIP

3 (10 ounce) packages frozen chopped
  broccoli, thawed
1/2 cup sliced mushrooms
2 (10 3/4 ounce) cans cream of chicken soup
2 (3 ounce) packages cream cheese with
  chives and garlic

In slow cooker, combine all ingredients. Mix well.
Cover. Cook on low 2 to 3 hours. Stir after 1 hour.
Serve with crackers, chips, or corn tortillas.

PUMPKIN BUTTER SPREAD

1 (15 ounce) can pumpkin
1 cup apple, peeled, grated
1/2 cup packed brown sugar
3/4 teaspoon pumpkin pie spice
1 cup apple juice

In slow cooker, combine all ingredients. Mix well.
Cover. Cook on high 1 1/2 hours. Reduce heat to low.
Cook 5 to 6 hours. Makes 3 cups.

REUBEN SPREAD

    1/2 pound chopped cooked corned beef
    1   (16 ounce) can sauerkraut, rinsed,
         drained
    3/4 cup Thousand Island salad dressing
    2   cups shredded Swiss cheese
    1   (3 ounce) package cream cheese, cubed

In slow cooker, combine all ingredients. Mix well.
Cover. Cook on low for 2 to 3 hours. Serve with
cocktail rye bread slices.

CHICKEN CHEESE SPREAD

    2   (12 1/2 ounce) cans white chicken, drained
    2   (8 ounce) packages cream cheese, softened
    1 1/2 cups mayonnaise
    1/2 cup diced green onion
    1/2 cup diced red bell pepper

In slow cooker, combine all ingredients. Mix well.
Cover. Cook on low 2 to 3 hours. Serve with
crackers. Makes 8 to 10 servings.

CRAB CHEESE SPREAD

2 cups flaked crabmeat
2 (8 ounce) packages cream cheese, softened
1½ cups mayonnaise
½ cup chopped green onion
1 cup shredded Swiss cheese

In slow cooker, combine all ingredients. Mix well. Cover. Cook on low 2 to 3 hours. Serve with crackers. Makes 8 to 10 servings.

HAVING A PARTY CHEESE BALL

2 (8 ounce) packages cream cheese
4 cups shredded cheddar cheese
4 tablespoons diced onion
4 tablespoons apple juice
1 cup chopped pecans

In slow cooker, add cream cheese. Cover. Cook on low until cheese melts. Mix in cheddar cheese, onion, and apple juice until smooth. Cover. Cook on low 1 hour. Pour mixture into medium bowl. Chill slightly. Form into ball. Roll in pecans. Serve with assorted crackers. Makes 12 to 15 servings.

NACHOS

- 1 pound ground beef, browned, drained
- 1 (19 ounce) can black beans, rinsed, drained
- 1 (1 ounce) package dry onion soup mix
- 1 cup salsa
- 1 (8½ ounce) package tortilla chips
- 1 cup shredded cheddar cheese

In slow cooker, combine beef, beans, soup mix, and salsa. Mix well. Cover. Cook on low 3 to 4 hours. Arrange tortilla chips on platter. Spread beef mixture over chips. Sprinkle with cheese.

NUTS ABOUT WALNUTS

- 4 cups walnuts
- ½ cup butter, melted
- 2½ tablespoons sugar
- 1 teaspoon allspice
- 1 teaspoon cinnamon

In slow cooker, add walnuts. Pour butter over nuts. Mix well. Cover. Cook on low 2 hours. Remove cover. Cook 30 minutes. Sprinkle nuts with sugar and spices. Mix well. Pour on cookie sheet to cool. Makes 6 to 8 servings.

JALAPEÑO COCKTAIL WIENERS

1 (10½ ounce) jar jalapeño jelly
1 (10 ounce) jar chili sauce
2 (16 ounce) packages smoked cocktail
    wieners

In slow cooker, combine jelly and chili sauce.
Mix well. Add wieners. Mix well. Cover. Cook on
low 3 to 4 hours.

SWEET AND SOUR COCKTAIL WIENERS

2 cups ketchup
¾ cup orange juice
¾ cup packed brown sugar
2 tablespoons mustard
1 tablespoon minced onion
1 pound cocktail wieners

In slow cooker, combine all ingredients except
cocktail wieners. Mix well. Add cocktail wieners.
Mix well. Cover. Cook on low 3 to 4 hours.

GOTTA HAVE HOT DOG ROLL UPS

2 (16 ounce) packages hot dogs, cut in half
1 pound bacon, cut in half
2 tablespoons brown sugar

Wrap each hot dog piece with bacon, sticking a toothpick through bacon and hot dog to hold. Place in bottom of slow cooker. Sprinkle with brown sugar. Cover. Cook on low 3 to 4 hours.

LITTLE SMOKIES LINKS

2 cups barbecue sauce
1/2 cup ketchup
1/2 cup packed brown sugar
2 tablespoons diced onion
2 (16 ounce) packages smoked cocktail wieners

In slow cooker, combine all ingredients. Mix well. Cover. Cook on low 3 to 4 hours. Makes 10 servings.

BUDGET PARTY LINKS

    2 (16 ounce) packages hot dogs, sliced
      1 inch thick
    2 cups barbecue sauce
  1/4 cup packed brown sugar
    1 teaspoon dry mustard
    2 tablespoons maple syrup

In slow cooker, combine all ingredients. Mix well.
Cover. Cook on low 3 to 4 hours. Makes 10 to 12
servings.

BBQ COCKTAIL WIENERS

   36 cocktail wieners
 2 1/2 cups barbecue sauce
    1 teaspoon dry mustard
  1/4 cup packed brown sugar

In slow cooker, combine all ingredients. Cover.
Cook on low 3 to 4 hours or high 1 1/2 to 2 hours.
Makes 6 to 8 servings.

PARTY COCKTAIL WIENERS

  2 (16 ounce) packages cocktail wieners
  1 cup ketchup
  1 cup barbecue sauce
  1 cup brown sugar
½ teaspoon Worcestershire sauce

In slow cooker, combine all ingredients. Cover. Cook on high 1½ hours. Remove lid and cook on low an additional 1 hour. Makes 8 to 10 servings.

SPICY HONEY WINGS

  1 (1½ ounce) envelope dry onion soup mix
½ cup honey
  1 tablespoon spicy brown mustard
18 chicken wings, separated at joints, tips discarded

In slow cooker, place chicken wings. In small bowl, combine onion soup mix, honey, and mustard. Mix well. Pour mixture over wings. Mix well. Cover. Cook on low 6 to 8 hours. Makes 18.

SAUCY SWEET CHICKEN WINGS

- 12 chicken wings, separated at joints, tips discarded
- 3 cups barbecue sauce
- 1/4 cup maple syrup
- 1/4 cup ketchup
- 1 tablespoon sugar

In slow cooker, place chicken wings. In medium bowl, combine remaining ingredients. Mix well. Pour mixture over wings. Cover. Cook on low 6 to 8 hours or high 3 to 4 hours. Makes 12.

BARBECUE CHICKEN WINGS

2½ pounds chicken wings, separated at
      joints, tips discarded
  1 cup barbecue sauce
  2 tablespoons maple syrup
  1 teaspoon sugar
  1 teaspoon Worcestershire sauce

In slow cooker, place chicken wings. In small
bowl, combine barbecue sauce, maple syrup,
sugar, and Worcestershire sauce. Pour mixture
over wings. Cover. Cook on low 6 to 8 hours.

SO GOOD CHICKEN WINGS

½ cup soy sauce
½ cup packed dark brown sugar
12 large chicken wings, separated at joints,
      tips discarded

In small bowl, combine soy sauce and brown sugar.
Mix well. Let set 10 minutes. Coat each wing with
mixture and place in slow cooker. Cover. Cook on
low 6 to 8 hours or high 3 to 4 hours. Makes 12
servings.

FIVE-SPICE CHICKEN WINGS

3 pounds chicken wings (about 16), separated at joints, tips discarded
1 cup bottled plum sauce
2 tablespoons butter, melted
1 teaspoon five-spice powder
Thin orange wedges and pineapple slices

Place wings in a single layer on foil-lined 15×10×1-inch baking pan. Bake in a 375°F oven for 20 minutes. Drain. Place wings in slow cooker. In small bowl, stir together plum sauce, melted butter, and five-spice powder. Pour mixture over wings, stirring to coat. Cover. Cook on low 4 to 5 hours or high 2 to 2½ hours. Serve immediately or keep warm on low up to 2 hours. Garnish with orange wedges and pineapple slices.

Better Homes and Gardens®
Test Kitchen

JUST WING IT

3 pounds chicken wings, separated at joints, tips discarded
1 cup honey
2 cups barbecue sauce

In slow cooker, place chicken wings. In small bowl, combine remaining ingredients. Mix well. Pour mixture over wings. Cover. Cook on low 6 to 8 hours.

SMOKE 'N HOT WINGS

2½ pounds chicken wings, separated at
    joints, tips discarded
 2 cups chili sauce
½ cup hot pepper sauce

In slow cooker, place chicken wings. In small
bowl, combine remaining ingredients. Mix well.
Pour mixture over wings. Cover. Cook on low 6 to 8
hours or high 3 to 4 hours.

PARTY TIME MEATBALLS

 2 (18 ounce) packages frozen precooked
    meatballs
 1 (12 ounce) jar savory beef gravy
 1 (1 ounce) package dry onion soup mix

In slow cooker, place meatballs. In medium bowl,
combine gravy and onion soup mix. Mix well. Add
mixture to meatballs. Cover. Cook on low 6 to 8
hours. Makes 72 meatballs.

BARBECUED MEATBALLS

  1 (36 ounce) package frozen precooked
      meatballs
  3 cups barbecue sauce
$1/3$ cup packed brown sugar
$1/4$ cup ketchup

In slow cooker, combine all ingredients.
Mix well. Cover. Cook on low 6 to 8 hours.
Makes 72 meatballs.

BEEF BURGER BITES

1	pound ground beef, browned, drained
2	tablespoons ketchup
2	teaspoons instant minced onion
1	teaspoon mustard
2	cups cubed American cheese
24	miniature sandwich buns

Coat inside slow cooker with nonstick cooking spray. In slow cooker, combine beef, ketchup, onion, and mustard. Mix well. Top with cheese. Cover. Cook on low 3 to 4 hours. Serve on miniature buns. Makes 24 appetizers.

PRETZEL TWIST NIBBLERS

1	(14 ounce) package pretzel nuggets
3	cups tiny twist shape pretzels
1/3	cup vegetable oil
1	(1 ounce) envelope ranch dressing mix

In slow cooker, add pretzels. In small bowl, combine oil and ranch dressing. Pour mixture over pretzels. Mix well. Cook on low 3 hours. Remove lid. Stir. Cook 30 additional minutes. Pour on cookie sheet to cool. Makes 6 to 8 servings.

SWISS CHEESE FONDUE

1 (16 ounce) package shredded Swiss cheese
1 cup apple juice
1 (10¾ ounce) can cheddar cheese soup
¼ teaspoon garlic salt

In slow cooker, combine all ingredients. Mix well. Cover. Cook on low 2 to 3 hours. Stir after 1 hour of cooking. Serve with vegetables, bread chunks, and fruit. Makes 4 cups.

CHEDDAR CHEESE FONDUE

1 (16 ounce) package cheddar cheese cubes
½ cup apple cider
½ teaspoon hot pepper sauce

Coat inside slow cooker with nonstick cooking spray. Add ingredients. Mix well. Cover. Cook on low 2 to 3 hours. Serve with French bread cubes, tortilla chips, or fresh vegetables.

Confetti Chicken Chili, page 90

Almost Like Mom's Potato Soup, page 60

SOUPS, STEWS, & CHILI

CREAMY BROCCOLI SOUP

1 small onion, chopped
1 tablespoon butter
1 (20 ounce) package frozen broccoli
2 (10¾ ounce) cans cream of celery soup
1 (10¾ ounce) can cream of mushroom soup
1 cup shredded American cheese
2 soup cans milk

In medium skillet, sauté onion in butter over medium heat. Place in slow cooker. Add broccoli, celery soup, mushroom soup, cheese, and milk. Cover. Cook on low 3 to 4 hours. Makes 6 to 8 servings.

BROCCOLI CHEESE SOUP

8 ounces Velveeta® cheese
2 (10¾ ounce) cans cream of celery soup
1 pint half-and-half
1 (10 ounce) package frozen
   chopped broccoli

In slow cooker, combine all ingredients. Cover. Cook on low 2 to 3 hours. Makes 4 to 6 servings.

CHEESY BROCCOLI SOUP

1 (16 ounce) package chopped frozen
   broccoli, thawed
1 (8 ounce) jar Cheese Whiz®
1 (10¾ ounce) can cream of celery soup
1 (16 ounce) carton half-and-half

In slow cooker, combine all ingredients. Mix well.
Cover. Cook on low 2 to 3 hours. Makes 6 servings.

BROCCOLI CHEDDAR CHEESE SOUP

1 (8 ounce) package shredded cheddar cheese
1 pint half-and-half
1 (10 ounce) package frozen broccoli

In slow cooker, combine all ingredients. Cover.
Cook on low 2 to 3 hours. Makes 6 servings.

CHEDDAR CHEESE SOUP

2 (10¾ ounce) cans cheddar cheese soup
1½ soup cans water
½ cup chopped tomatoes
¼ cup chopped green chiles

In slow cooker, combine all ingredients.
Mix well. Cover and cook on low 2 to 3 hours.
Makes 4 servings.

BROCCOLI AND CHEESE SOUP

2 (16 ounce) packages chopped broccoli
2 (10¾ ounce) cans cheddar cheese soup
2 (12 ounce) cans evaporated milk
¼ cup finely chopped onion
½ teaspoon salt

In slow cooker, combine all ingredients. Cover.
Cook on low 4 to 6 hours. Makes 8 servings.

CHEESY CHEDDAR SOUP

- 2 (10¾ ounce) cans cream of mushroom soup
- 1 pound cheddar cheese, cubed
- 1 cup evaporated milk
- 1 teaspoon Worcestershire sauce
- ¼ teaspoon paprika

In slow cooker, combine all ingredients. Mix well.
Cover. Cook on low 3 to 4 hours. Makes 4 servings.

VEGETABLE SOUP

- 4 cups vegetable broth
- 3 cups water
- 2 (8 ounce) cans tomato sauce
- 2 cups dried pasta
- 2½ cups frozen vegetables, thawed
- Salt and pepper

In slow cooker, combine all ingredients. Mix well.
Cover. Cook on low 8 to 9 hours or high 3 to 4
hours. Makes 4 to 6 servings.

MORE THAN CHICKEN SOUP

2 (10¾ ounce) cans cream of chicken soup
1 cup broccoli florets, thawed
1 cup cooked chicken cubes
1¾ cups milk

In slow cooker, combine all ingredients. Mix well.
Cover. Cook on low 2 to 3 hours. Makes 4 servings.

GET A GRIP ONION SOUP

3 large onions, sliced
3 tablespoons butter or margarine, melted
3 tablespoons all-purpose flour
1 tablespoon Worcestershire sauce
1 teaspoon sugar
4 (14 ounce) cans beef broth

In slow cooker, combine onions and butter. Cover.
Cook on high 40 minutes. In small bowl, combine
flour, Worcestershire sauce, and sugar. Add
mixture and broth to onions. Stir well. Cover. Cook
on low heat 7 to 9 hours. Makes 8 servings.

ON THE GO ONION SOUP

3 pounds onions, sliced
½ cup butter
2 (14 ounce) cans beef broth
1 can water

In large skillet, sauté onions in butter until lightly golden brown. Pour onions into slow cooker. Add remaining ingredients. Cover. Cook on low 8 to 10 hours. If desired, top each serving with shredded mozzarella cheese. Makes 4 to 6 servings.

EASY FIX'N BEEF SOUP

1 pound ground beef, browned, drained
2 cups beef broth
2 cups tomato juice
1 (16 ounce) package frozen mixed vegetables
1 teaspoon salt

In slow cooker, combine all ingredients. Mix well. Cover. Cook on low 4 to 6 hours. Makes 4 servings.

LITTLE BITE BEEF SOUP

- 2 pounds stewing beef, cut in ½-inch chunks
- 2 (15 ounce) cans black beans, drained
- 2 cups frozen corn
- 2 cups chopped onion
- 2 (16 ounce) jars chunky salsa
- 4 cups water
- 2 teaspoons ground cumin
- 1 teaspoon red pepper

In slow cooker, combine all ingredients.
Mix well. Cover. Cook on low 8 to 10 hours.
Makes 10 to 12 servings.

CHILL OUT BEEF SOUP

- 1 (2.5 ounce) jar mushrooms, drained
- ¼ green bell pepper, diced
- 1 tablespoon butter or margarine
- 1 (10¾ ounce) can beef soup
- 2 (10¾ ounce) cans beef noodle soup
- 1½ soup cans water

In slow cooker, combine all ingredients. Cover.
Cook on low 3 to 4 hours. Makes 4 to 6 servings.

SPAGHETTI-LOVER'S SOUP

- 1 pound lean ground beef
- 1 medium onion, chopped
- 1 small green sweet pepper, chopped
- 1 stalk celery, chopped
- 1 medium carrot, chopped
- 2 cloves garlic, minced
- 2 (14.5 ounce) cans no-salt-added diced tomatoes, undrained
- 1 (14 ounce) jar spaghetti sauce
- 1 cup water
- 1 tablespoon quick-cooking tapioca, crushed
- 1/2 teaspoon dried Italian seasoning, crushed
- 1/4 teaspoon salt
- 1/4 teaspoon black pepper
- 1/8 teaspoon cayenne pepper
- 2 ounces dried spaghetti, broken into 2-inch pieces

In large skillet, cook ground beef, onion, sweet pepper, celery, carrot, and garlic over medium heat until meat is browned and vegetables are tender. Drain. Place meat mixture in slow cooker. Stir in all remaining ingredients, except spaghetti. Cover. Cook on low 8 to 10 hours or high 4 to 5 hours. If using low-heat setting, turn to high and stir in spaghetti. Cover. Cook an additional 15 to 20 minutes until pasta is tender.

Better Homes and Gardens

Test Kitchen

VEGGIE BEEF SOUP

- 1/2 pound extra lean ground beef, browned, drained
- 1 (14 ounce) can beef broth
- 1 (14.5 ounce) can stewed tomatoes, chopped, undrained
- 1 cup frozen mixed vegetables
- 1 (8 ounce) can tomato sauce
- 1/3 cup uncooked quick-cooking barley

In slow cooker, combine all ingredients. Cover. Cook on low 4 to 6 hours. Makes 4 to 5 servings.

GROUND BEEF SOUP

- 1 pound lean ground beef, browned, drained
- 2 1/2 cups tomato juice
- 1 1/2 cups beef broth
- 3 cups frozen mixed vegetables

In slow cooker, combine all ingredients. Cover. Cook on low 4 to 6 hours. Makes 4 to 6 servings.

NO FUSS VEGGIE BEEF SOUP

1 pound ground beef, browned, drained
2 cups tomato juice
2 cups beef broth
1 (16 ounce) package frozen mixed vegetables

In slow cooker, combine all ingredients. Cover.
Cook on low 3 to 4 hours. Makes 4 to 5 servings.

BUTTER BEAN SOUP

1 pound butter beans
6 cups water
1 teaspoon salt
1/2 cup butter
1 cup cubed ham

In slow cooker, add beans and water. Cover. Cook on
low 8 to 10 hours. Add salt, butter, and ham.
Cover. Cook an additional 1 hour. Makes 6 servings.

MEATBALL SOUP

1 (16 ounce) package frozen precooked meatballs
2 (14 ounce) cans beef broth
2 (14 ounce) cans diced Italian-seasoned tomatoes, undrained
1 cup water
1 (16 ounce) package frozen mixed vegetables

In slow cooker, combine meatballs, broth, tomatoes, and water. Cover. Cook on low 6 to 8 hours. Add vegetables. Cover. Cook an additional 1 hour. Makes 6 servings.

MAMA MIA'S MEATBALL SOUP

1 (16 ounce) package frozen precooked meatballs
2 (10¾ ounce) cans garlic mushroom soup
2 soup cans water

In slow cooker, combine all ingredients. Cover. Cook on low 4 to 5 hours. Makes 4 to 6 servings.

TERRIFIC TOMATO SOUP

  1   cup chopped onion
  2   cloves garlic, minced
  1   tablespoon olive oil
  9   medium tomatoes, chopped

In large saucepan, sauté onion and garlic in olive oil over medium heat until golden brown. Pour into slow cooker. Stir in tomatoes. Cover. Cook on low 6 to 8 hours. Season to taste with salt and pepper. Makes 4 to 6 servings.

CREAMY TOMATO SOUP

  1   (28 ounce) can diced tomatoes, undrained
  1   (26 ounce) jar tomato pasta sauce
  2   (14 ounce) cans chicken broth
  1   cup sour cream
 ½   cup milk

In slow cooker, combine tomatoes, pasta sauce, and chicken broth. Cover. Cook on low 4 to 6 hours. Add sour cream and milk. Mix well. Cover. Cook an additional 15 minutes. Makes 8 servings.

CURRY TOMATO SOUP

- 1 (46 ounce) can tomato juice
- 1/4 cup sugar
- 1/4 cup butter or margarine
- 1 teaspoon curry powder
- 1/4 teaspoon onion powder
- 1/4 cup flour

In slow cooker, combine all ingredients, except flour. Cover. Cook on low 3 to 4 hours. In small bowl, place 2 cups tomato soup mixture. Add flour slowly. Mix well. Add flour mixture to slow cooker. Mix well. Cover. Cook an additional 20 to 30 minutes. Makes 6 servings.

CHILI SOUP

- 1 pound Italian sausage
- 1 onion, chopped
- 1 (14 1/2 ounce) can diced tomatoes, undrained
- 2 cups vegetable tomato juice
- 1 (15 1/2 ounce) can Mexican-style chili beans
- 1 teaspoon chili powder

In large skillet, brown sausage and onion over medium high heat. Drain. In slow cooker, combine all ingredients. Mix well. Cover. Cook on low 5 to 6 hours. Makes 6 to 8 servings.

LENTIL AND HAM SOUP

- 1 cup reduced-sodium chicken broth
- 1 cup water
- 1 stalk celery, chopped
- 1 medium carrot, thinly sliced
- 1/3 cup brown lentils, rinsed and drained
- 1/3 cup diced cooked ham
- 1/2 of a small onion, cut into thin wedges
- 1/2 teaspoon dried thyme, crushed
- 1 cup shredded fresh spinach

In slow cooker, combine broth, water, celery, carrot, lentils, ham, onion, and thyme. Cover and cook on low 7 to 8 hours or high 3 1/2 to 4 hours. Just before serving, stir in spinach. Makes 2 servings.

Better Homes and Gardens

Test Kitchen

TURKEY & VEGETABLE SOUP

- 2 pounds ground turkey, cooked, drained
- 2 (14 ounce) cans beef broth
- 1 (28 ounce) can chopped tomatoes, undrained
- 1 (16 ounce) package mixed frozen vegetables
- 1/2 cup uncooked barley
- 1 teaspoon salt
- 1/2 teaspoon pepper

In slow cooker, combine all ingredients.
Mix well. Cover. Cook on high 4 to 6 hours.
Makes 6 to 8 servings.

ITALIAN POTATO SOUP

- 5 medium potatoes, sliced thin
- 1/2 cup diced onion
- 1 1/4 pounds Italian sausage, formed into bite-sized pieces
- 2 1/2 teaspoons salt
- 1 1/2 teaspoons pepper
- 6 cups water
- 1/4 cup butter
- 2 cups milk

In slow cooker, layer 1/2 of potatoes, onion,
sausage, salt, and pepper. Repeat layering. Add
water and butter. Cover. Cook on low 10 hours. Add
milk. Mix well and serve. Makes 6 to 8 servings.

GERMAN POTATO SOUP

1   pound cooked smoked sausage, halved
    lengthwise and cut into ½-inch slices
1   (14 ounce) package frozen diced hash brown
    potatoes with onions and peppers (about 4
    cups)
1   (16 ounce) jar sauerkraut, rinsed, drained
2   tablespoons stone-ground mustard
3   (14 ounce) cans chicken broth
    Shredded red cabbage or thinly sliced
    red onion

In slow cooker, place sausage, frozen potatoes,
sauerkraut, and mustard. Pour broth over mixture
in cooker. Cover. Cook on low 7 to 9 hours or high
3½ to 4½ hours. Top each serving with red
cabbage or red onion. Makes 6 to 8 servings.

Better
Homes
and Gardens®
Test Kitchen

THICK POTATO SOUP

- 2 pounds potatoes, cut into 1-inch cubes
- 2 (10¾ ounce) cans cream of mushroom soup
- 1 cup sliced green onion
- ⅛ teaspoon red pepper
- 1½ cups shredded cheddar cheese
- 1 cup sour cream
- 1 cup milk

In slow cooker, combine potatoes, soup, green onion, and red pepper. Mix well. Cover. Cook on low 8 to 10 hours or high 4 hours. Add cheese, sour cream, and milk. Mix until cheese melts. Cover. Cook an additional 15 minutes. Makes 6 servings.

ALMOST LIKE MOM'S POTATO SOUP

- 1 (5 ounce) package scalloped potato mix
- 4 cups chicken broth
- 1 onion, chopped
- 2 cups half-and-half
- ⅓ cup flour

In slow cooker, combine scalloped potato mix, broth, and onion. Cover. Cook on low 4 to 6 hours. In medium bowl, combine half-and-half and flour. Mix until smooth. Pour flour mixture into slow cooker slowly, stirring constantly. Cover. Cook an additional 1 hour, stirring occasionally. Makes 5 servings.

SMASHED POTATO SOUP

3½	pounds potatoes, cut into ¾-inch cubes
½	cup chopped yellow and/or red sweet pepper
1½	teaspoons bottled roasted garlic
½	teaspoon ground black pepper
4½	cups chicken broth
½	cup whipping cream, half-and-half, or light cream
1	cup shredded cheddar cheese
½	cup thinly sliced green onion
	Sliced green onion

In slow cooker, combine potatoes, sweet pepper, garlic, and black pepper. Pour broth over all. Cover. Cook on low 8 to 10 hours or high 4 to 5 hours. Mash potatoes slightly with a potato masher. Stir in whipping cream, cheddar cheese, and the ½ cup thinly sliced green onion. Top individual servings with additional sliced green onion.

Better
Homes
and Gardens®

Test Kitchen

BEEF POTATO SOUP

1 pound lean ground beef, browned, drained
4 cups cubed potatoes
1 cup chopped onion
3 (8 ounce) cans tomato sauce
1½ teaspoons salt
Water

In slow cooker, combine beef, potatoes, onion, tomato sauce, and salt. Add water to cover ingredients. Mix well. Cover. Cook on low 8 to 10 hours. Makes 6 to 8 servings.

POTATO AND CARROT SOUP

4 medium red potatoes, cubed
2 carrots, diced
1 onion, chopped
1 stalk celery, chopped
2 (14 ounce) cans chicken broth with garlic
2 strips bacon, cooked, crumbled
1 cup instant mashed potato flakes
1 cup milk

In slow cooker, combine potatoes, carrots, onion, celery, broth, and bacon. Mix well. Cover. Cook on low 8 to 10 hours. Add potato flakes and milk. Mix well. Makes 4 servings.

SWEET POTATO SOUP

$2\frac{1}{2}$ to 3 pounds sweet potatoes, peeled and cut into 1-inch pieces
$\frac{1}{2}$ cup chopped onion
$\frac{1}{4}$ cup maple syrup
1 clove garlic, minced
$\frac{1}{2}$ teaspoon dried sage, crushed
$\frac{1}{4}$ teaspoon salt
$\frac{1}{8}$ teaspoon ground black pepper
2 (14 ounce) cans chicken broth
1 cup water
$\frac{1}{2}$ cup half-and-half, light cream, or milk
Crisp-cooked crumbled bacon
Sliced green onion

In slow cooker, combine potatoes, onion, syrup, garlic, sage, salt, and pepper. Pour broth and water over all. Cover. Cook on low 6 to 8 hours or high 3 to 4 hours. Using a potato masher, mash the soup until desired consistency. Whisk in half-and-half until well mixed. Sprinkle each serving with crumbled bacon and green onion. Makes 6 servings.

Better Homes and Gardens®
Test Kitchen

MINESTRONE SOUP

2 (14 ounce) cans chicken broth
1 (14 ounce) can crushed tomatoes
1 (14½ ounce) can kidney beans
1½ cups frozen mixed vegetables
3 teaspoons Italian seasoning

In slow cooker, combine all ingredients. Cover.
Cook on low 3 to 4 hours. Makes 4 to 5 servings.

CHEESY POTATO SOUP

4 medium potatoes, cooked, cubed
1 small onion, chopped
1 (10¾ ounce) can cheddar cheese soup
1 (10¾ ounce) can cream of celery soup
2 cups milk
1 teaspoon salt

In slow cooker, combine all ingredients. Cover.
Cook on low heat 2½ to 3 hours. Makes 4 to 6
servings.

SANTA FE SOUP

1	cup dried red kidney beans, sorted, rinsed
1¼	pounds beef stew meat, cut into bite-sized pieces
1	(15.25 ounce) can whole kernel corn, drained
1	(14.5 ounce) can diced tomatoes, undrained
1	(1.25 ounce) package taco seasoning mix
1	(4.5 ounce) can chopped green chiles
1½	cups water
1	onion, chopped

In large bowl, place beans. Cover with 3 cups water for 8 hours or overnight. Drain beans. In slow cooker, combine all ingredients. Mix well. Cover. Cook on low 8 to 10 hours. Makes 6 servings.

TORTELLINI SOUP

1	(28 ounce) can diced tomatoes, undrained
1	(15.5 ounce) can great northern beans, drained, rinsed
2	(14½ ounce) cans chicken broth
2	medium zucchini, halved, cut into 1-inch slices
1	onion, finely chopped
1	(8 ounce) package uncooked cheese-filled tortellini

In slow cooker, combine all ingredients, except tortellini. Mix well. Cover. Cook on low 6 to 8 hours. Add tortellini. Cover. Cook on high an additional 20 minutes. Makes 8 servings.

SAUSAGE AND TORTELLINI SOUP

- 2 (14.5 ounce) cans Italian-style tomatoes
- 3 cups water
- 2 cups frozen cut green beans or Italian green beans
- 1 (10.5 ounce) can condensed French onion soup
- 8 ounces cooked smoked turkey sausage, halved lengthwise and cut into 1/2-inch slices
- 2 cups packaged shredded cabbage with carrot (coleslaw mix)
- 1 (9 ounce) package refrigerated cheese-filled tortellini
  Shaved Parmesan cheese

In slow cooker, combine undrained tomatoes, water, frozen green beans, onion soup, and turkey sausage. Cover. Cook on low 8 to 10 hours or high 4 to 5 hours. If using low-heat setting, turn to high and stir in cabbage and tortellini. Cover. Cook an additional 15 minutes. Top each serving with Parmesan cheese. Makes 10 to 12 servings.

Better Homes and Gardens®
Test Kitchen

SAVORY BEAN AND SPINACH SOUP

- 3 (14 ounce) cans vegetable broth
- 1 (15 ounce) can tomato puree
- 1 (15 ounce) can white or Great Northern beans, rinsed and drained
- 1/2 cup converted rice
- 1/2 cup finely chopped onion
- 2 cloves garlic, minced
- 1 teaspoon dried basil, crushed
- 1/4 teaspoon salt
- 1/4 teaspoon ground black pepper
- 8 cups coarsely chopped fresh spinach or kale leaves
  Finely shredded Parmesan cheese

In slow cooker, combine broth, tomato puree, beans, rice, onion, garlic, basil, salt, and pepper. Cover. Cook on low 5 to 7 hours or high 2½ to 3½ hours. Stir spinach into soup. Serve with Parmesan cheese. Makes 6 servings.

Better Homes and Gardens
Test Kitchen

BELL PEPPER SOUP

1½ pounds lean ground beef, browned, drained
3 green bell peppers, chopped
1 onion, chopped
1 (28 ounce) can crushed tomatoes, undrained
2 (14½ ounce) cans beef broth
2 (10¾ ounce) cans tomato soup
1 cup instant rice, uncooked
1 cup water

In slow cooker, combine all ingredients. Mix well.
Cover. Cook on low 6 to 8 hours. Makes 8 servings.

LAZY LASAGNA SOUP

1 pound ground beef, browned, drained
1 (14½ ounce) can diced tomatoes, undrained
1 (7¾ ounce) package lasagna dinner mix
1 (7 ounce) can whole kernel corn, undrained
5 cups water
1 small zucchini, chopped
½ cup chopped onion
2 tablespoons grated Parmesan cheese

In slow cooker, combine all ingredients. Cover.
Cook on low 6 to 8 hours. Makes 8 to 10 servings.

NACHO CHEESE CHICKEN CHOWDER

1 pound skinless, boneless chicken breast halves, cut into $\frac{1}{2}$-inch pieces
2 (14.5 ounce) cans Mexican-style tomatoes
1 (10$\frac{3}{4}$ ounce) can nacho cheese soup
1 (10 ounce) package frozen whole kernel corn
  Shredded Mexican-style or cheddar cheese

In slow cooker, stir together chicken, undrained tomatoes, soup, and corn. Cover. Cook on low 4 to 5 hours or high 2 to 2$\frac{1}{2}$ hours. Sprinkle each serving with cheese. Makes 6 servings.

Better Homes and Gardens®
Test Kitchen

CORN CHOWDER

- 4 medium potatoes, peeled, diced
- 2 (14$\frac{1}{2}$ ounce) cans diced tomatoes, undrained
- 2 (15$\frac{1}{4}$ ounce) cans whole kernel corn, undrained
- 4 strips bacon, cooked, chopped
- 1 onion, chopped

In slow cooker, combine all ingredients. Cover. Cook on low 8 to 10 hours. Makes 8 to 9 servings.

ON THE ROAD CLAM CHOWDER

- 2 (10$\frac{3}{4}$ ounce) cans clam chowder soup
- 1 cup corn
- 2$\frac{1}{2}$ cups chopped cooked shrimp
- 1$\frac{3}{4}$ cups milk

In slow cooker, combine all ingredients. Cover. Cook on low 2$\frac{1}{2}$ to 3 hours, stirring often. Makes 4 servings.

BAYSIDE CLAM CHOWDER

3   (10¾ ounce) cans cream of potato soup
2   (10¾ ounce) cans clam chowder soup
½   cup butter
1   small onion, diced
1   pint half-and-half
2   (6½ ounce) cans clams, chopped

In slow cooker, combine all ingredients. Cover. Cook on low 3 to 4 hours. Makes 4 to 6 servings.

CHICKEN & WILD RICE SOUP

½   pound skinless, boneless chicken thighs, cut into bite-sized pieces
3   (14½ ounce) cans chicken broth
2   carrots, thinly sliced
⅔   cup uncooked wild rice
½   cup chopped onion
1½   cups frozen broccoli florets, thawed
1½   cups frozen corn, thawed

In slow cooker, combine chicken, broth, carrots, wild rice, and onion. Mix well. Cover. Cook on low 8 to 10 hours. Add broccoli and corn. Mix well. Cover. Cook on high an additional 10 minutes. Makes 6 servings.

MEXICAN SPLIT PEA SOUP

1 (16 ounce) package dried split peas, sorted, rinsed
4 cups water
6 ounces smoked chorizo sausage, sliced thin, casings removed
1 (10½ ounce) can chicken broth
1 (11 ounce) can Mexican-style whole kernel corn, drained
½ cup sliced green onion

In slow cooker, combine peas, water, sausage, and broth. Mix well. Cover. Cook on low 8 to 9 hours. Add corn and onion. Mix well. Cover. Cook on high an additional 10 minutes. Makes 6 servings.

LOUISIANA SHRIMP GUMBO

1 onion, chopped
1 green bell pepper, chopped
2 cloves garlic, minced
2 tablespoons vegetable oil
3 (10¾ ounce) cans golden mushroom soup
1 (24 ounce) jar salsa with corn and beans
2 pounds frozen peeled small shrimp, thawed

In medium skillet, sauté onion, pepper, and garlic in oil over medium high heat until lightly golden. Pour mixture into slow cooker. In slow cooker, add soup and salsa. Mix well. Cover. Cook on low 2 hours. Add shrimp. Mix well. Cover. Cook an additional 1 to 2 hours. Makes 6 to 8 servings.

NOODLE LOVERS SOUP

1 pound lean ground beef, browned, drained
1 (14.5 ounce) can diced tomatoes, undrained
1 (1.15 ounce) package dry beefy mushroom
  soup mix
3 cups water
1 onion, chopped
1 celery stalk, sliced thin
2 cups frozen mixed vegetables, thawed
1 cup uncooked fine egg noodles

In slow cooker, combine beef, tomatoes, soup mix,
water, onion, and celery. Mix well. Cover. Cook on
low 6 to 8 hours. Add vegetables and noodles. Mix
well. Cover. Cook on high an additional 20
minutes. Makes 6 servings.

BEEFY NOODLE SOUP

1 pound ground beef, browned, drained
1 (46 ounce) can V8® juice
1 (16 ounce) package frozen mixed vegetables
1 (1 ounce) package onion soup mix
1 (3 ounce) package beef ramen noodles with
  flavor packet

In slow cooker, combine all ingredients.
Mix well. Cover. Cook on low for 5 to 6 hours.
Makes 8 servings.

CHICKEN DUMP SOUP

2 (14½ ounce) cans chicken broth
1 (14¾ ounce) can cream-style corn
1 (10 ounce) package frozen chopped broccoli
2 (5 ounce) cans chunk chicken, drained
1 (2 ounce) jar diced pimientos, drained

In slow cooker, combine all ingredients. Mix well.
Cover. Cook on low 4 hours. Makes 4 servings.

BEANS WITH BACON SOUP

10 cups chicken broth
3 (15 ounce) cans great northern beans,
drained
1 (14½ ounce) can diced tomatoes, undrained
1 (10 ounce) package frozen diced carrots
1 pound bacon, cooked, crumbled
1 onion, chopped
2 cloves garlic, minced

In slow cooker, combine all ingredients. Mix well.
Cover. Cook on low 6 to 8 hours. Makes 8 to 10
servings.

BLACK BEAN SOUP

3 (15 ounce) cans black beans, rinsed, drained
2 (14½ ounce) cans chicken broth
1 (14½ ounce) can diced stewed tomatoes, undrained
2 cups chopped onion
2 cups chopped green bell pepper
2 cloves garlic, minced

In slow cooker, combine all ingredients. Mix well. Cover. Cook on low 8 to 10 hours or high 5 hours. Makes 8 servings.

ALPHABET SOUP

½ pound beef stew meat, diced
1 (14½ ounce) can Italian-style diced tomatoes
1 (8 ounce) can tomato sauce
3 cups water
1 (16 ounce) packaged frozen mixed vegetables
3 teaspoons instant beef bouillon
½ cup alphabet noodles, uncooked

In slow cooker, combine all ingredients, except noodles. Mix well. Cover. Cook on low 6 to 8 hours. Add noodles. Cover. Cook on high an additional 20 minutes. Makes 3 to 4 servings.

LEFTOVER CHICKEN AND VEGETABLE SOUP

3 (14 ounce) cans chicken broth
2 cups cooked diced chicken
2 cups frozen whole kernel corn
1 (10 ounce) package frozen cut green beans
2 tomatoes, diced
1 stalk celery, chopped
¼ teaspoon garlic powder

In slow cooker, combine all ingredients. Mix well.
Cover. Cook on low 4 to 6 hours. Makes 6 servings.

SAUSAGE SOUP

4 (14½ ounce) cans chicken broth
8 red potatoes, diced
1 (1 ounce) package Italian salad
   dressing mix
1 pound Italian sausage, browned, drained
2 cups frozen chopped spinach, thawed

In slow cooker, combine broth, potatoes, and
dressing mix. Cover. Cook on low 8 to 10 hours.
Add sausage and spinach. Mix well. Cover. Cook
an additional 15 minutes. Makes 8 to 10 servings.

NEW MEXICO STEW

- 1 pound lean ground beef, browned, drained
- 1 pound Velveeta® Mexican-style cheese, cubed
- 1 (15 ounce) can ranch-style beans, undrained
- 1 cup frozen whole kernel corn
- 1½ cups water

In slow cooker, combine all ingredients. Cover. Cook on low 4 to 6 hours. Makes 4 to 6 servings.

GREEN CHILE STEW

- 6 medium potatoes, peeled, cubed
- 2 pounds lean pork roast, cubed
- 2 teaspoons salt
- 1 teaspoon pepper
- ⅛ cup minced onion
- 1 (7 ounce) can chopped green chiles
- 4 cloves garlic, minced
  Water

In slow cooker, layer potatoes then pork. Sprinkle with salt and pepper. Top with onion, green chiles, and garlic. Add enough water to cover ingredients. Cover. Cook on low 10 to 12 hours. Makes 8 to 10 servings.

BEEF GREEN CHILE STEW

- 2 pounds round steak, cubed
- 1 clove garlic, minced
- 2 large onions, chopped
- 2 (7 ounce) cans chopped green chiles
- 5 (10 ounce) cans tomatoes with green chiles
- 2 cups water
- 1/4 cup beef broth

In large skillet with little oil, cook steak, garlic, and onions over low heat until lightly browned. Place in slow cooker. Add remaining ingredients. Mix well. Cook on low 10 to 12 hours. Serve with warm tortillas. Makes 8 servings.

SAUSAGE & BEANS STEW

- 1 (16 ounce) package smoked sausage, cut in 1-inch slices
- 1/3 cup diced onion
- 2 (15 ounce) cans kidney beans, undrained
- 1 (15 ounce) can pinto beans, undrained
- 1 (10 ounce) can diced tomatoes, undrained
- 1 (10¾ ounce) can minestrone soup

In slow cooker, combine all ingredients. Mix well. Cover. Cook on low 6 to 8 hours or high 3 to 4 hours. Makes 6 to 8 servings.

HOT TEX-MEX STEW

1½ **pounds stewing beef, cubed**
2 **cups salsa**
1 **cup barbecue sauce**
½ **cup chopped onion**
2 **cups corn**
1 **(15 ounce) can pinto beans, rinsed, drained**
¼ **cup chopped cilantro**

In slow cooker, combine all ingredients. Mix well.
Cover. Cook on low 8 to 10 hours or high 4 to 5
hours. Makes 6 servings.

FIX & GO STEW

2½ pounds stewing beef, cubed
3 carrots, sliced
1 small onion, sliced
3 large potatoes, sliced
3 stalks celery, sliced
2 cups chopped tomatoes
2 (10¾ ounce) cans tomato soup

In slow cooker, combine all ingredients. Mix well. Cover. Cook on low 8 to 10 hours. Salt and pepper to taste. Makes 6 servings.

CABBAGE PATCH STEW

2 pounds stewing beef, cubed, browned
6 cups shredded cabbage
½ cup corn
3 carrots, sliced
1 small onion, chopped
1½ cups beef broth
2 (15 ounce) cans chopped tomatoes, undrained
Salt and pepper

In slow cooker, combine all ingredients. Mix well. Cover. Cook on low 8 to 10 hours or high 3 to 4 hours. Makes 4 to 6 servings.

STEW ON IT

- 2 pounds boneless beef chuck, cut into 1-inch cubes
- 1/4 cup flour
- 1 1/3 cups sliced carrots
- 1 (16 ounce) can whole tomatoes, undrained, chopped
- 1 (1 ounce) package dry onion soup mix
- 1/2 cup water
- 1 cup sliced mushrooms

In slow cooker, toss beef with flour. Add carrots, tomatoes, soup mix, and water. Cover. Cook on low 8 to 10 hours. Add mushrooms. Cover. Cook an additional 10 minutes. Makes 8 servings.

BEEF STEW

- 1 pound stew meat, cut into bite-sized pieces
- 2 potatoes, peeled, cubed
- 3 carrots, sliced
- 1 onion, sliced
- 1 1/2 teaspoons Italian seasoning
- 2 cups beef broth

In slow cooker, combine all ingredients. Cover. Cook on low 8 to 10 hours. Makes 4 to 6 servings.

BEEFY MUSHROOM STEW

1½ pounds beef stew meat, cut into bite-
    sized pieces
1   (10¾ ounce) can cream of mushroom soup
3   (4 ounce) cans sliced mushrooms, drained
½   cup beef broth
1   (1 ounce) package dry onion soup mix

In slow cooker, combine all ingredients. Mix well.
Cover. Cook on low 6 to 8 hours. Makes 6 servings.

TEXAS BEEF STEW

2   pounds stew meat
1   (28 ounce) can whole tomatoes, undrained
1   cup small frozen whole onions
1   teaspoon chili powder
1   (1¼ ounce) package taco seasoning mix
1   (15 ounce) can black beans, rinsed,
    drained
1   (11 ounce) can corn with red and green bell
    peppers, drained

In slow cooker, combine beef, tomatoes, onions,
and chili powder. Cover. Cook on low 8 to 10 hours.
Stir in taco seasoning, beans, and corn. Cover.
Cook on high 30 minutes. Makes 6 servings.

HEARTY BEEF STEW

1 pound lean ground beef
2 cloves garlic, minced
1 (16 ounce) package frozen vegetables
2 cups southern-style hash brown potatoes
1 (14 ounce) jar marinara sauce
1 (10½ ounce) can beef broth
1 tablespoon Worcestershire sauce

In large skillet, brown beef with garlic over medium heat. Drain. In slow cooker, add beef, vegetables, potatoes, sauce, beef broth, and Worcestershire sauce. Cover. Cook on low 4 to 6 hours or high 1½ to 2 hours. Makes 4 to 6 servings.

BEEF SIRLOIN STEW

1 tablespoon vegetable oil
1 pound beef sirloin, cut into thin strips, browned
1 (16 ounce) package frozen potatoes, carrots, celery, and onions
1 (12 ounce) jar beef gravy

In slow cooker, combine all ingredients. Mix well. Cover. Cook on low 3 to 4 hours or high 1½ to 2 hours.

PORK STEW

1½   pounds boneless pork shoulder roast,
     cut into bite-sized pieces, browned
8   small red potatoes, quartered
2   cups halved baby carrots
1   (12 ounce) jar pork gravy
¼   cup ketchup
½   teaspoon poultry seasoning
1½   cups frozen green beans, thawed

In slow cooker, combine all ingredients, except green beans. Mix well. Cover. Cook on low 6 to 8 hours. Add green beans. Mix well. Cover. Cook an additional 20 minutes. Makes 6 servings.

CHICKEN STEW

1   pound skinless, boneless chicken pieces,
     cut into bite-sized pieces
4   medium potatoes, peeled, cubed
1   (14½ ounce) can Italian-style tomatoes
2   onions, chopped
1   green bell pepper, chopped
2   cloves garlic, minced
½   cup chicken broth
1   teaspoon Italian seasoning

In slow cooker, layer chicken and potatoes. In large bowl, combine remaining ingredients. Mix well. Pour mixture over chicken and potatoes. Cover. Cook on low 8 to 10 hours. Makes 6 servings.

CHICKEN CHILI

2 pounds chicken, cut into bite-sized pieces
2 (14½ ounce) cans Mexican-style diced
  tomatoes, undrained
1 (15 ounce) can tomato sauce
1 (1¼ ounce) package mild chili
  seasoning mix
2 (15½ ounce) cans hominy

Place chicken in slow cooker. In medium bowl,
combine tomatoes, tomato sauce, and seasoning.
Pour over chicken. Cover. Cook on low 8 to 10
hours. Add hominy, stir well. Cover. Cook an
additional 20 minutes. Makes 6 servings.

HURRY UP CHILI

½ pound ground beef, browned, drained
2 (14.5 ounce) cans stewed tomatoes,
  undrained, chopped
2 (15 ounce) cans spicy chili beans,
  undrained
2 teaspoons chili powder

In slow cooker, combine all ingredients. Mix well.
Cover. Cook on low 3 to 4 hours or high 1½ hours.
Makes 6 servings.

EVERYDAY CHILI

- 1 pound ground beef, browned, drained
- 1/2 cup chopped onion
- 2 (15 ounce) cans chili with beans
- 1 (10 ounce) can diced tomatoes with green chiles

In slow cooker, combine all ingredients. Mix well. Cover. Cook on low 4 to 6 hours or on high 1½ to 2 hours. Makes 6 servings.

QUICK DRAW CHILI

- 1½ pounds lean ground beef, browned, drained
- 3 links sausage with cheddar, sliced
- 2 (15 ounce) cans Cajun-style mixed vegetables, undrained
- 1 (14½ ounce) can diced tomatoes, undrained
- 2 (10¾ ounce) cans tomato soup

In slow cooker, combine all ingredients. Mix well. Cover. Cook on low 4 to 6 hours or high 2 hours. Makes 8 to 10 servings.

OUT ALL DAY CHILI

1 pound ground beef
½ pound Italian sausage
½ cup chopped onion
1 (28 ounce) can tomato sauce
1 teaspoon chili powder
1 (15 ounce) can spicy chili beans, undrained
1 (15 ounce) can kidney beans, rinsed, drained
1 teaspoon honey

In large skillet, cook beef and sausage over medium heat until brown. Drain. Place mixture into slow cooker. Add remaining ingredients. Mix well. Cover. Cook on low 6 to 8 hours. Makes 6 servings.

SLOW COOKED CHILI

2 pounds ground beef
2 tablespoons chili powder
1 tablespoon cumin
½ cup diced onion
1 (28 ounce) can crushed tomatoes
1 cup water
2 (15 ounce) cans red kidney beans, rinsed, drained
2 tablespoons hot pepper sauce

In large skillet, cook beef, chili powder, cumin, and onion over medium heat until browned. Drain. Place mixture into slow cooker. Add remaining ingredients. Mix well. Cover. Cook on low 6 to 8 hours. Makes 6 to 8 servings.

CHILI CON CARNE

  1   pound lean ground beef, browned, drained
 1/2 cup chopped onion
1 1/2 teaspoons chili powder
  1   (15 ounce) can Mexican-style tomatoes
  1   (15 ounce) can kidney beans, undrained

In slow cooker, combine all ingredients. Mix well. Cover. Cook on low 4 to 6 hours. Makes 4 servings.

CHICKEN CHILI MADE SPECIAL

  1   (18 ounce) package barbecue sauce with
     shredded chicken
  2   (15 ounce) cans black beans, rinsed,
     drained
  1   (28 ounce) can crushed tomatoes, undrained
  1   (14 ounce) can beef broth
  1   (1.25 ounce) package taco seasoning
  1   teaspoon chili powder

In slow cooker, combine all ingredients. Mix well. Cover. Cook on low 4 to 6 hours. Top with sour cream or cheese (optional). Makes 6 to 8 servings.

CHILI DOGS 'N ONE POT

1 (16 ounce) package hot dogs
2 (15 ounce) cans chili without beans
1/2 cup chopped onion

In slow cooker, combine all ingredients. Mix well. Cover. Cook on low 3 to 4 hours. Serve with hot dog buns. Makes 10 servings.

CHUNKY CHILI

2 (15 ounce) cans chili without beans
1 (16 ounce) package small hot dogs
1 (8 ounce) package American cheese, cubed
1/2 cup thick and chunky salsa

In slow cooker, combine all ingredients. Mix well. Cover. Cook on low 4 to 6 hours or high 1 1/2 to 2 hours. Makes 6 to 8 servings.

CONFETTI CHICKEN CHILI

3	(15 ounce) cans Great Northern, pinto, and/or white cannellini beans
1½	cups chopped sweet red, green and/or yellow peppers
1	cup coarsely shredded carrots
½	cup sliced scallions
2	cloves garlic, chopped
2	teaspoons dried oregano
1	teaspoon ground cumin
½	teaspoon salt
2	(14 ounce) cans chicken broth
2½	cups shredded or chopped cooked chicken or turkey
	Shredded Monterey Jack cheese

Drain and rinse two cans of the beans and place in slow cooker. Use a potato masher or fork to mash beans. Drain and rinse the remaining can of beans (do not mash). Stir beans, sweet peppers, carrots, scallions, garlic, oregano, cumin, and salt into mashed beans. Add chicken broth. Mix well. Cover. Cook on low 6 to 8 hours or high 3 to 4 hours. If necessary, raise temperature to high-heat setting and stir chicken into chili. Cover. Cook an additional 15 minutes until chicken is heated through. Sprinkle each serving with cheese.

Better Homes and Gardens®
Test Kitchen

FIX-AND-FORGET WHITE CHILI

- 12 ounces skinless, boneless chicken breast halves, cubed
- 1 tablespoon cooking oil
- 3 (15 ounce) cans Great Northern beans or navy beans, rinsed and drained
- 2½ cups chicken broth
- 2 (4 ounce) cans chopped green chiles
- 1 medium onion, chopped
- 1½ teaspoons cumin seeds
- 1½ teaspoons bottled minced garlic (3 cloves)
- ¼ to 1 teaspoon cayenne pepper
- ¼ teaspoon salt
  Dairy sour cream
  Avocado slices
  Fresh thyme sprigs

In large skillet, cook chicken in hot oil just until lightly brown. Place beans in slow cooker; mash slightly with a potato masher. Add chicken to beans. Stir in chicken broth, undrained chiles, onion, cumin seeds, garlic, cayenne pepper, and salt. Cover and cook on low 7 to 8 hours or high 3½ to 4 hours. Serve with sour cream and avocado and garnish with thyme sprigs. Makes 6 servings.

Better Homes and Gardens®
Test Kitchen

IN-YOUR-SLEEP CHILI

- 1 pound ground beef
- 1 large onion, chopped
- 2 (15 ounce) cans chili beans in chili gravy
- 1 (14½ ounce) can diced tomatoes with green chiles, undrained
- 1 (11½ ounce) can hot-style vegetable juice
  Sliced green onion, dairy sour cream, and/or shredded cheddar cheese

In large skillet, cook ground beef and onion until meat is brown. Drain. In slow cooker, combine ground beef mixture, beans, undrained tomatoes, and vegetable juice. Cover. Cook on low 4 to 6 hours or on high 2 to 3 hours. If desired, top each serving with green onion, sour cream, and/or cheddar cheese. Makes 6 servings.

Better Homes and Gardens®
Test Kitchen

Easy Vegetable Dish, page 97

Bean-and-Rice-Stuffed
Peppers, page 180

VEGETABLES, PASTA, CASSEROLES, & RICE

CAULIFLOWER & BROCCOLI

1   (12 ounce) package frozen cauliflower, thawed
1   (10 ounce) package frozen broccoli, thawed
1   (10¾ ounce) can cheddar cheese soup
4   slices bacon, cooked, crumbled

In slow cooker, place cauliflower and broccoli. Pour soup over vegetables. Sprinkle bacon on top. Cover. Cook on low 2½ to 3 hours. Makes 6 servings.

BROCCOLI, CAULIFLOWER & CHEESE

1   (16 ounce) package frozen cauliflower
2   (10 ounce) packages frozen broccoli
½ cup water
1   tablespoon butter or margarine
2   cups shredded cheddar cheese

In slow cooker, combine all ingredients. Mix well. Cover. Cook on low 3 to 4 hours. Makes 6 to 8 servings.

I'LL BRING THE CAULIFLOWER

8   cups cauliflower florets
1   large onion, thinly sliced
1   (16 ounce) jar cheddar cheese pasta sauce

In slow cooker, combine all ingredients.
Mix well. Cover. Cook on low 6 to 8 hours
or high 3 hours. Makes 10 to 12 servings.

CHEDDAR & BROCCOLI

- 6 cups cooked broccoli cuts
- 2 (10¾ ounce) cans cheddar cheese soup
- ¾ cup milk
- 1 cup French fried onions

In slow cooker, combine all ingredients.
Mix well. Cover. Cook on low 3 to 4 hours.
Makes 6 to 8 servings.

CHEESE & BROCCOLI

- 1 (10¾ ounce) can cheddar cheese soup
- ¼ cup milk
- 4 cups frozen broccoli cuts

In slow cooker, combine all ingredients. Mix well.
Cover. Cook on low 3 to 4 hours or high 1½ hours.
Makes 4 servings.

BROCCOLI

6 cups fresh broccoli florets
1½ cups water
1 (1 ounce) package dry onion soup mix
1 tablespoon olive oil

In slow cooker, combine all ingredients. Mix well.
Cover. Cook on low 3 to 4 hours. Makes 4 servings.

EASY VEGETABLE DISH

2 (16 ounce) packages frozen mixed
vegetables, thawed
1 cup French fried onions
1 (16 ounce) package shredded American
cheese
¼ cup milk

In slow cooker, combine all ingredients.
Mix well. Cover. Cook on low 3 to 4 hours.
Makes 6 to 8 servings.

PEAS AU GRATIN

- 3 cups peas
- 1 (2½ ounce) can water chestnuts, drained, sliced
- 1 (10¾ ounce) can cream of mushroom soup
- 1 cup shredded cheddar cheese

Coat inside slow cooker with nonstick cooking spray. In slow cooker, combine all ingredients. Mix well. Cover. Cook on low 4 to 6 hours. Makes 6 servings.

SIDE DISH CABBAGE

- 1 medium head cabbage, cut in chunks
- 3 slices raw bacon
- ⅓ cup butter or margarine
- ½ cup hot water
  Salt and pepper

In slow cooker, combine all ingredients. Mix well. Cover. Cook on high 1 hour. Uncover. Mix well. Cover. Reduce heat to low. Cook 2 hours. Makes 6 servings.

ITALIAN ZUCCHINI

1	red onion, sliced
1	green bell pepper, sliced
4	medium zucchini, sliced
1	(14$\frac{1}{2}$ ounce) can chopped Italian-style tomatoes
$\frac{1}{4}$	cup shredded Parmesan cheese
1	tablespoon butter or margarine, melted

In slow cooker, layer onion, pepper, zucchini, and tomatoes. Sprinkle cheese over zucchini mixture. Drizzle butter over cheese. Cover. Cook on low 3 hours or high 1$\frac{1}{2}$ hours. Makes 6 servings.

SAUCY STUFFED PEPPERS

- 1 pound lean ground beef, browned, drained
- 2/3 cup bread crumbs
- 1 egg
- 1/2 teaspoon Italian seasoning
- 1 (32 ounce) jar spaghetti sauce, divided
- 5 green bell peppers, halved

In large bowl, combine beef, bread crumbs, egg, seasoning, and 1 cup spaghetti sauce. Mix well. In slow cooker, arrange peppers. Spoon beef mixture into pepper halves. Pour remaining spaghetti sauce over peppers. Cover. Cook on low 6 to 8 hours. Makes 5 servings.

CABBAGE & HAM

- 1/4 cup water
- 1 medium-size cabbage, cut into quarters
- 1/4 cup melted butter or margarine
- 4 pounds fully cooked ham
  Salt and pepper

In slow cooker, pour water. Place cabbage on top of water. Drizzle butter over cabbage. Add ham. Cover. Cook on low 6 to 8 hours. Salt and pepper to taste. Makes 6 servings.

SOUTHERN STYLE CABBAGE

    1   medium head green cabbage, thinly sliced
    1   small onion, thinly sliced
    ½   teaspoon salt
    2   slices bacon
    ½   cup water

In slow cooker, combine all ingredients, except
water. Mix well. Pour water over mixture. Cover.
Cook on low 4 to 6 hours. Makes 6 servings.

CABBAGE

    1   head cabbage, chopped
    ¼   cup water
    2   tablespoons olive oil
    1   clove garlic, minced
    1   teaspoon soy sauce

In slow cooker, place cabbage. In small bowl, combine
remaining ingredients. Pour over cabbage. Cover. Cook
on low 4 to 6 hours. Makes 4 to 6 servings.

CREAMED CORN

2 (16 ounce) packages frozen whole kernel corn
4 (3 ounce) packages cream cheese, cubed
1 cup milk
1/2 cup butter or margarine, melted
2 teaspoons sugar
1/2 teaspoon salt
1/4 teaspoon pepper

In slow cooker, place corn. Top with cream cheese. In small bowl, combine remaining ingredients. Mix well. Pour mixture over corn. Cover. Cook on high 3 to 4 hours. Makes 8 to 10 servings.

CORN & GREEN CHILE DISH

1 (15 ounce) can corn, drained
1 (15 ounce) can creamed corn, undrained
1 (8 ounce) package cream cheese, softened
1 (4 ounce) can chopped green chiles

Coat inside slow cooker with nonstick cooking spray. In large bowl, combine all ingredients. Mix well. Pour mixture into slow cooker. Cover. Cook on low 3 to 4 hours. Makes 8 servings.

ALFREDO GREEN BEANS

2	(9 ounce) packages or 1 (20 ounce) package frozen cut green beans (about 5 cups)
1½	cups chopped red sweet pepper
1	(10 ounce) container refrigerated light Alfredo sauce
1	cup chopped onion
1	(8 ounce) can sliced water chestnuts, drained
¼	teaspoon garlic salt
½	cup Parmesan-flavor croutons, slightly crushed

Lightly coat inside of slow cooker with nonstick cooking spray. In large bowl, combine green beans, sweet pepper, Alfredo sauce, onion, water chestnuts, and garlic salt. Place bean mixture into slow cooker. Cover. Cook on low 5 to 6 hours or high 2½ to 3 hours. Serve with a slotted spoon. Sprinkle each serving with crushed croutons. Makes 8 servings.

Better Homes and Gardens®

Test Kitchen

DON'T BAKE IT GREEN BEANS

- 2 (1¾ ounce) cans cream of mushroom soup
- ¾ cup milk
- 2 teaspoons soy sauce
- 8 cups green beans
- 1 cup French fried onions

In slow cooker, combine all ingredients. Mix well. Cover. Cook on low 4 to 6 hours. Makes 8 servings.

BIT SPECIAL GREEN BEANS

- 1 (12 ounce) package frozen cut green beans
- 1 (8 ounce) can sliced water chestnuts, drained
- ½ cup roasted bell pepper strips (from a jar)
- 1 (10 ounce) container refrigerated Alfredo sauce
- 1 cup French fried onions

In slow cooker, combine all ingredients. Mix well. Cover. Cook on low 3 hours. Uncover. Mix well. Cover. Cook an additional 1 hour. Makes 6 to 8 servings.

SAUCY GREEN BEANS AND POTATOES

2 pounds new potatoes, large ones halved
1 pound fresh green beans, trimmed and halved crosswise
1 (10¾ ounce) can condensed cream of celery soup
¾ cup water
¼ cup Dijon-style mustard
¾ teaspoon dried dill weed

Place potatoes and green beans in slow cooker. In medium bowl, combine soup, water, mustard, and dill weed. Pour over vegetables. Mix gently. Cover. Cook on low 6 to 8 hours or on high 3 to 4 hours. Stir gently before serving. Makes 12 servings.

Better Homes and Gardens®

Test Kitchen

JUST BEEF & BEANS

- 1 pound lean ground beef, browned, drained
- 2 (10¾ ounce) cans cream of mushroom soup
- 1 cup shredded cheddar cheese
- 2 (15 ounce) cans green beans, drained

In slow cooker, combine all ingredients.
Mix well. Cover. Cook on low 4 to 6 hours.
Makes 4 to 6 servings.

VEGGIE DISH

- 4 cups green beans
- 4 cups corn
- ½ cup sour cream
- 1 (10¾ ounce) can cream of chicken soup
- ½ cup shredded mild cheddar cheese

In large bowl, combine all ingredients. Mix well.
Pour mixture into slow cooker. Cover. Cook on
low 4 to 6 hours. Makes 8 to 10 servings.

MUSTARD GLAZED CARROTS

12   carrots, sliced
1/2 cup packed brown sugar
1/3 cup Dijon mustard

In slow cooker, combine all ingredients. Cover.
Cook on low 4 to 6 hours or high 2 to 3 hours.
Makes 8 to 10 servings.

SWEET ORANGE CARROTS

1 1/2 pounds carrots, peeled, sliced
1 1/2 cups orange juice
    1 tablespoon sugar
    3 tablespoons maple syrup
  1/3 cup butter, melted

In slow cooker, place carrots. In medium bowl,
combine juice, sugar, syrup, and butter. Mix well.
Pour mixture over carrots. Cover. Cook on low
4 to 6 hours. Makes 6 servings.

CANDIED CARROTS

2 (16 ounce) packages frozen sliced carrots
1 (6 ounce) bottle maple syrup
1/4 cup packed brown sugar

In slow cooker, combine all ingredients.
Mix well. Cover. Cook on low 6 to 7 hours.
Makes 8 to 10 servings.

MAPLE GLAZED SQUASH

1 large butternut squash, cut into chunks
2 tablespoons butter, melted
1/3 cup maple syrup
1/4 cup packed brown sugar

In slow cooker, place squash. Drizzle butter,
pour syrup, and sprinkle brown sugar over squash.
Cover. Cook on low 6 to 8 hours. Makes 6 servings.

GEE WHIZ HOMINY

    2   (15½ ounce) cans hominy, drained
    1   onion, chopped
    1   (10¾ ounce) can cream of mushroom soup
    1   (8 ounce) jar jalapeño Cheese Whiz®
    ½   cup evaporated milk
    2   cups crushed corn chips

In slow cooker, combine all ingredients, except corn chips. Mix well. Cover. Cook on low 4 to 6 hours. Top with corn chips. Cover. Cook an additional 15 minutes. Makes 6 servings.

TASTY CORN ON THE COB

    6   medium ears corn
    ½   cup melted butter

Place each ear of corn on a piece of heavy-duty aluminum foil. Brush butter over corn. Wrap. Place corn in slow cooker. Cover. Cook on high 2 hours or low 4 to 6 hours. Makes 6 servings.

SAUCY CORN & BROCCOLI

  1   (16 ounce) package frozen cut broccoli
  1   (16 ounce) package frozen corn
  1   (10¾ ounce) can cream of chicken soup
1½ cups shredded American cheese
¼ cup milk

Spray inside of slow cooker with nonstick cooking spray. In slow cooker, combine all ingredients. Mix well. Cover. Cook on low 3 to 4 hours or high 2 hours. Makes 8 to 10 servings.

GARLIC VEGETABLES

4 medium potatoes, thinly sliced
4 medium carrots, sliced
1 (1 ounce) package herb and garlic soup mix
⅓ cup water
1 tablespoon olive oil

In slow cooker, combine all ingredients. Cover. Cook on low 6 to 8 hours. Makes 4 servings.

STEWED TOMATOES

6	large tomatoes, skinned, diced
1/2	cup butter
1	teaspoon salt
1/2	teaspoon pepper
1/2	cup fresh basil

In slow cooker, place tomatoes. Cover. Cook on high 1 hour. Add remaining ingredients. Mix well. Cover. Reduce heat to low and cook an additional 1½ hours. Makes 6 to 8 servings.

NOW THAT'S A BAKED POTATO

8	to 10 medium unpeeled potatoes
2	tablespoons vegetable oil

Pierce potatoes with fork. Place potatoes and oil in large plastic food storage bag. Toss to coat with oil. Wrap potatoes individually in aluminum foil. Place in slow cooker without water. Cover. Cook on low heat 8 to 10 hours or until potatoes are tender. Makes 8 to 10 servings.

ALFREDO TOPPED BAKED POTATOES

6	baking potatoes
1	(4½ ounce) jar sliced mushrooms
2	cups frozen green peas, thawed
1	(7 ounce) jar roasted red peppers, drained, sliced
2½	cups Alfredo sauce
¾	cup milk

Scrub and pierce potatoes. Wrap each potato in aluminum foil. Place in slow cooker without water. Cover. Cook on low 7 to 10 hours or high 3 to 4 hours. In medium saucepan, combine remaining ingredients. Mix well. Cook over medium heat until hot and bubbly. Cut and open potatoes. Put mixture on top of potatoes. Makes 6 servings.

POTATOES SURPRISE

5	medium baked potatoes, cooked, sliced
2	(10¾ ounce) cans broccoli cheese soup
¾	cup milk
1	small onion, sliced
1	cup shredded cheddar cheese

In slow cooker, combine all ingredients. Mix well. Cover. Cook on low 4 to 6 hours. Makes 6 servings.

SATURDAY NIGHT POTATO SKINS

```
6   to 8 potatoes
½   cup butter, melted
6   to 8 strips bacon, cooked, crumbled
½   cup salsa
1   (8 ounce) package shredded cheddar cheese
```

Prick potatoes with fork and wrap in aluminum foil. Place in slow cooker without water. Cover. Cook on low 8 to 10 hours. Slice potatoes in half. Scoop out potatoes, leaving one-fourth of potato on skin. Drizzle with butter. Top potatoes with bacon, salsa, and cheese. Place on cookie sheet. Broil 10 to 15 minutes or until cheese melts. Makes 6 to 8 servings.

SAUSAGE & POTATOES DINNER

```
1   (20 ounce) package refrigerated new
    potato wedges
1   medium green bell pepper, chopped
1   (16 ounce) package smoked sausage, sliced
1   cup barbecue sauce
```

In slow cooker, combine all ingredients. Mix well. Cover. Cook on low 4 to 6 hours. Makes 4 servings.

CHEDDAR POTATOES

  2   pounds russet potatoes, peeled, diced
  1   cup water
1/3 cup butter
1/2 to 3/4 cup milk
1/2 cup finely chopped green onion
  3   ounces shredded cheddar cheese
     Salt and pepper

In slow cooker, add potatoes and water. Dot potatoes with butter. Cover. Cook on low 6 to 8 hours or high 3 hours. In large bowl, place potatoes and remaining ingredients. Salt and pepper to taste. Mix with electric mixer. Makes 8 servings.

MASHED RED POTATOES

  3   pounds small (2 to 3 inches) red
     potatoes, halved
  4   cloves garlic, minced
1/2 cup water
  2   tablespoons olive oil
  1   teaspoon salt
1/2 cup chive and onion cream cheese, softened
1/4 to 1/2 cup milk

In slow cooker, place potatoes, garlic, water, olive oil, and salt. Mix well. Cover. Cook on low 8 to 10 hours or high 4 to 5 hours or until potatoes are tender. Mash potato mixture with fork or potato masher. Add cream cheese and enough milk for desired consistency. Serve immediately, or reduce heat to low for up to 2 hours.

CHEESY TATERS

4   medium potatoes, peeled, sliced thin
1   cup shredded cheddar cheese
1   ($10^3/_4$ ounce) can cream of mushroom soup
$1/_2$ teaspoon pepper
$1/_2$ teaspoon paprika

In slow cooker, place potatoes. Sprinkle cheese over potatoes. In small bowl, mix soup, pepper, and paprika. Pour over potatoes and cheese. Cover. Cook on low 6 to 8 hours or high 3 to 4 hours.

CHEESY STEAK FRIES

2   ($10^3/_4$ ounce) cans cheddar cheese soup
$1/_2$ cup milk
$1/_2$ teaspoon garlic powder
$1/_4$ teaspoon onion powder
8   cups frozen steak fries

In slow cooker, combine all ingredients. Mix well. Cover. Cook on low 3 to 4 hours or high $1^1/_2$ to 2 hours. Makes 6 to 8 servings.

DELICIOUS CREAMY POTATOES

2½ pounds small red potatoes, quartered
1 (8 ounce) container sour cream
1 (0.4 ounce) package buttermilk ranch
   dressing mix
1 (10¾ ounce) can cream of mushroom soup
½ cup water

In slow cooker, combine all ingredients. Mix well.
Cover. Cook on low 8 to 10 hours or high 3½ hours.
Makes 6 servings.

EXTRA CHEESY HASH BROWNS

1 (32 ounce) package frozen hash brown
   potatoes
1 cup shredded cheddar cheese
2 (10¾ ounce) cans cheddar cheese soup
1 (2.8 ounce) can French fried onion rings

Coat inside slow cooker with nonstick cooking
spray. Add all ingredients. Mix well. Cover. Cook
on low 4 to 6 hours or high 2 to 3 hours. Makes 8
servings.

HOT GERMAN POTATO SALAD

- 2 pounds potatoes, peeled and cut into ¼-inch-thick slices (about 6 cups)
- 1 cup chopped onion
- 1 cup chopped celery
- ¾ cup water
- ⅔ cup cider vinegar
- ¼ cup sugar
- 1 tsp. salt
- ¾ tsp. celery seeds
- ¼ tsp. ground black pepper
- 6 slices bacon, crisp-cooked, drained, and crumbled
- ¼ cup snipped fresh parsley
- 1 (10 ounce) bag prewashed spinach
  Snipped fresh dill

In slow cooker, combine potatoes, onion, and celery. In a bowl, combine water, vinegar, sugar, salt, celery seeds, and pepper. Pour over potato mixture. Cover. Cook on low 8 to 10 hours or high 4 to 5 hours. Stir in bacon and parsley. Spoon the hot mixture over fresh spinach leaves. Garnish with snipped dill. Stir gently before serving. Makes 12 servings.

Better Homes and Gardens®

Test Kitchen

IT'S SO CHEESY POTATO HASH BROWNS

1   (32 ounce) package frozen hash brown potatoes
2   (10¾ ounce) cans Mexican-style cheddar
    cheese soup
1   (12 ounce) can evaporated milk
2   cups crushed cheddar cheese flavored
    crackers, divided
2   cups shredded cheddar cheese

In slow cooker, combine potatoes, soup, milk, and half of crackers. Mix well. Cover. Cook on low 6 to 8 hours. Sprinkle remaining crackers and cheese over potato mixture. Cover. Cook an additional 15 minutes. Makes 4 to 6 servings.

SOUPER HASH BROWNS

1   (32 ounce) package frozen shredded
    hash browns
2   cups shredded cheddar cheese
2   cups diced ham
1   (12 ounce) can evaporated milk
1   (10¾ ounce) can cream of potato soup

Coat inside slow cooker with nonstick cooking spray. In large bowl, combine all ingredients. Mix well. Pour mixture in slow cooker. Cover. Cook on low 6 to 8 hours or high 2½ to 3 hours. Makes 4 to 6 servings.

CLASSIC POTATOES

1 (10¾ ounce) can cheddar cheese soup
¾ cup milk
½ cup grated Parmesan cheese
4 medium potatoes, cut in 1-inch pieces
½ cup French fried onions

In slow cooker, combine all ingredients.
Mix well. Cover. Cook on low 6 to 8 hours or
high 3 to 4 hours. Makes 4 servings.

RANCH POTATOES

2 (24 ounce) packages frozen hash brown
potatoes, partially thawed
2 (8 ounce) packages cream cheese, softened
2 (⅞ ounce) packages Ranch dressing mix
2 (10¾ ounce) cans cream of potato soup

In slow cooker, place hash browns. In medium bowl,
combine remaining ingredients. Pour mixture over
hash browns. Cover. Cook on low 6 to 8 hours. Stir
before serving. Makes 8 to 12 servings.

SOUTHERN STYLE POTATOES

1   (32 ounce) package frozen southern-style
    hash brown potatoes
2   (10³/4 ounce) cans cheddar cheese soup
1   (12 ounce) can evaporated milk
1   (2.8 ounce) can French fried onions,
    divided

In slow cooker, combine hash browns, soup, milk,
and half of the French fried onions. Mix well.
Cover. Cook on low 4 to 6 hours. Top with remaining
onions before serving. Makes 8 servings.

POTATOES & GRAVY WITH CHOPS

4   to 6 medium potatoes, quartered
4   to 6 pork chops
2   (12 ounce) jars brown gravy

In slow cooker, place potatoes. Arrange chops on
potatoes. Pour gravy over top. Cover. Cook on low
8 to 10 hours. Makes 4 to 6 servings.

SCALLOPED POTATOES, HAM & CHEESE

8   medium potatoes, peeled, thinly sliced
2   cups cubed ham
2   onions, diced
1   (10¾ ounce) can cream of mushroom soup
2   cups shredded cheddar cheese

In slow cooker, place half of potatoes, ham, onions, soup, and cheese. Repeat layering. Cover. Cook on low 8 to 10 hours. Makes 8 to 10 servings.

SCALLOPED POTATO BAKE

5   medium potatoes, sliced thin
1   small onion, sliced thin
2   (10¾ ounce) cans cream of celery soup
1   cup evaporated milk
1   tablespoon butter or margarine

In slow cooker combine all ingredients. Mix well. Cover. Cook on low 8 to 10 hours. Makes 6 servings.

SOUR CREAM SCALLOPED POTATOES & HAM

1   (28 ounce) bag frozen diced potatoes
1   cup shredded cheddar cheese
1   cup cubed American cheese
1   ($10^3/_4$ ounce) can cream of celery soup
2   (8 ounce) containers sour cream
1½ cups cubed ham

In slow cooker, combine all ingredients. Mix well. Cover. Cook on low 4 to 6 hours. Makes 8 servings.

SANTA FE STYLE SCALLOPED POTATOES & HAM

1   (32 ounce) package hash brown potatoes
2   tablespoons butter or margarine, melted
½   pound cooked diced ham
1   (12 ounce) container chive and onion sour cream potato topper
1   (11 ounce) can Mexican-style whole kernel corn, undrained
1   ($10^3/_4$ ounce) can cream of mushroom soup
2   cups water
1½ cups shredded cheddar cheese

In slow cooker, combine potatoes and butter. Mix well. Add remaining ingredients. Mix well. Cover. Cook on low 3 to 4 hours. Makes 6 servings.

SCALLOPED POTATOES & HAM

5	medium potatoes, sliced
2	cups chopped ham
4	tablespoons butter or margarine
3	tablespoons flour
1	teaspoon salt
2	cups milk
1	cup shredded cheddar cheese

In slow cooker, place potatoes and ham. In medium saucepan, melt butter over medium low heat. Add flour and salt; cook until bubbly. Add milk slowly, stirring until smooth and thickened. Add cheese. Mix well. Pour mixture over potatoes. Cover. Cook on low 8 to 10 hours or high 3 to 4 hours. Makes 6 servings.

SCALLOPED POTATOES & CHOPS

1	box scalloped potatoes
1/2	cup shredded cheddar cheese
4	pork chops, fat trimmed

Add ingredients required on package to make potatoes. Do not cook potatoes. Add cheese to potatoes. Mix well. In slow cooker, pour potato mixture. Place chops on potatoes. Cover. Cook on low 6 hours. Makes 4 servings.

SWEET POTATOES & HAM

4   sweet potatoes, sliced in half lengthwise
2   pounds boneless ham, cubed
1   cup maple syrup

In slow cooker, place potatoes. Top with ham.
Pour syrup over ham and potatoes. Cover. Cook
on low 6 to 8 hours. Makes 6 servings.

ORANGE SWEET POTATOES & PORK

4   medium sweet potatoes, sliced
6   boneless pork loin chops, browned
1   cup orange juice
1/3   cup packed brown sugar

In slow cooker, place sweet potatoes and pork loin.
In small bowl, combine orange juice and brown
sugar. Mix well. Pour mixture over top. Cover.
Cook on low 8 to 10 hours. Makes 6 servings.

ORANGE–SAGE SWEET POTATOES WITH BACON

- 4 pounds sweet potatoes, peeled and cut into 1/4-inch-thick slices
- 1/2 cup frozen orange juice concentrate, thawed
- 3 tablespoons packed brown sugar
- 1 1/2 teaspoons salt
- 1/2 teaspoon dried leaf sage, crushed
- 1/2 teaspoon dried thyme, crushed
- 2 tablespoons butter, cut up
- 4 slices bacon, crisp-cooked, crumbled

Place sweet potato slices in slow cooker. In small bowl, stir together orange juice concentrate, brown sugar, salt, sage, and thyme. Pour over sweet potato slices. Toss to coat. Dot with butter. Cover. Cook on low 5 to 6 hours or high 2 1/2 to 3 hours. Before serving, stir to coat with orange juice mixture and sprinkle with crumbled bacon. Makes 10 to 12 servings.

Better Homes and Gardens
Test Kitchen

SWEET POTATOES

2	pounds sweet potatoes, peeled, diced
1/2	cup butter
1/2	cup packed dark brown sugar
1	teaspoon ground cinnamon
1/2	teaspoon ground nutmeg
1	teaspoon vanilla

In slow cooker, combine all ingredients. Cover.
Cook on low 6 to 8 hours. Makes 8 servings.

CANDIED SWEET POTATOES

1 1/2	cups packed brown sugar
1/3	cup butter
1/4	cup maple syrup
1/4	cup water
8	sweet potatoes, cooked

In small saucepan, combine sugar, butter, syrup,
and water. Mix well. Cook over medium heat until
mixture starts to boil. Place sweet potatoes in
slow cooker. Pour mixture over potatoes. Cover.
Cook on low 3 to 4 hours or high 1 1/2 to 2 hours.
Makes 8 servings.

PEACHY PIE SWEET POTATOES

2¼	pounds sweet potatoes, peeled, cut into ½-inch slices
1	cup peach pie filling
3	tablespoons butter or margarine, melted, divided
½	teaspoon salt
2	tablespoons brown sugar
⅛	teaspoon cinnamon
½	cup chopped pecans

In slow cooker, combine potatoes, pie filling, 2 tablespoons butter, and salt. Mix well. Cover. Cook on low 6 to 8 hours or high 3 to 3½ hours. In small nonstick skillet over medium heat, sauté 1 tablespoon butter, brown sugar, cinnamon, and pecans for 3 minutes. Set aside to cool. Just before serving, stir potatoes. Top with pecan mixture and serve. Makes 8 to 10 servings.

REFRIED BEANS DISH

1	(15 ounce) can refried beans
½	cup chopped onion
⅓	cup chopped green bell pepper
3	eggs
1½	cups shredded cheddar cheese
½	teaspoon chili powder

In large bowl, combine all ingredients. Mix well. Pour mixture into slow cooker. Cover. Cook on low 3 to 4 hours. Makes 6 to 8 servings.

PORK & BEANS SUPPER

2 (15 ounce) cans pork and beans
2 cups cooked chopped pork
1/3 cup ketchup
1/4 cup packed brown sugar
1 teaspoon dry mustard

In slow cooker, combine all ingredients.
Mix well. Cover. Cook on low 4 to 6 hours or
high 1 1/2 to 2 hours. Makes 6 to 8 servings.

SHORTCUT BUTTER BEANS

2 (15 ounce) cans butter beans
2 slices uncooked bacon
1 tablespoon butter or margarine

In slow cooker, combine all ingredients.
Mix well. Cover. Cook on high 1 1/2 to 2 hours.
Makes 4 to 6 servings.

SHORTCUT BEANS & HAM

2 medium carrots, diced
1 onion, chopped
2 tablespoons butter or margarine
2¼ cups water
2 (15½ ounce) cans great northern beans,
   divided, rinsed, drained
1½ cups cubed cooked ham

In slow cooker, combine carrots, onion, butter,
and water. Cover. Cook on low 5 to 6 hours. Mash 1
can of beans; add to slow cooker. Add remaining
beans and ham. Mix well. Cover. Cook an additional
2 to 3 hours. Makes 6 servings.

BEANS, HAM & BUTTER

1 pound butter beans
5 cups water
2 cups chopped fully cooked ham
⅓ cup butter or margarine
1 teaspoon salt

In large pan, place beans. Cover with cold water
and soak overnight. Drain and rinse beans. Pour
beans in slow cooker. Pour 5 cups water over
beans. Add ham. Cover. Cook on low 8 to 10 hours.
Add butter, salt, and pepper. Let sit 5 minutes.
Makes 6 to 8 servings.

NAVY BEANS & HAM HOCK

2½   cups navy beans
 6   cups water
 1   ham hock
 1   teaspoon salt

In slow cooker, add beans and water. Let sit 2
hours. Add ham hock. Cover. Cook on low 8 to 10
hours. Add salt. Makes 6 to 8 servings.

CAJUN BEANS & SAUSAGE

 2   (15 ounce) cans kidney or pinto beans
 1   pound smoked sausage, cut into
     2-inch pieces
 2   teaspoons Cajun seasoning

In slow cooker, combine all ingredients.
Mix well. Cover. Cook on low 3 to 4 hours or
high 1½ to 2 hours. Serve with white rice.
Makes 4 to 6 servings.

CHUCK WAGON BBQ BEANS

2 pounds boneless pork stew meat, cubed
1/2 cup chopped onion
1 (16 ounce) bottle barbecue sauce, divided
2 (16 ounce) cans baked beans, drained
1 (14 1/2 ounce) can chopped stewed tomatoes
1/2 cup packed brown sugar
1/4 teaspoon chili powder

In slow cooker, combine pork, onion, and 1 cup barbecue sauce. Cover. Cook on low 6 to 8 hours or high 4 to 5 hours. Add remaining ingredients. Mix well. Cover. Cook on high an additional 30 minutes.

QUICK TRICK BAKE BEANS

2 (15 ounce) cans pork and beans
1/4 cup ketchup
1/4 cup maple syrup
1/2 cup sliced onion
2 tablespoons brown sugar

In slow cooker, combine all ingredients. Mix well. Cover. Cook on low 3 to 4 hours. Makes 6 to 8 servings.

TOUCHDOWN BAKED BEANS

1	(16 ounce) package dried navy beans, sorted, rinsed
11	cups water, divided
1/2	cup molasses
1/2	cup chopped onion
1/3	cup packed brown sugar
3	teaspoons dry mustard
1	teaspoon salt
1/2	teaspoon liquid smoke

In large soup pot over high heat, combine beans and 10 cups water. Bring to boil. Reduce heat. Cover and simmer 2 hours. Drain. In slow cooker, combine beans, 1 cup water, molasses, onion, brown sugar, dry mustard, salt, and liquid smoke. Cover. Cook on low 10 to 12 hours. Makes 10 servings.

ROUTE 66 BAKED BEANS

2	(15 ounce) cans pork and beans
3 1/2	tablespoons Worcestershire sauce
1/2	cup barbecue sauce
1/2	teaspoon dry mustard
1/4	cup diced onion

In slow cooker, combine all ingredients. Mix well. Cover. Cook on low 4 to 6 hours or high 1 1/2 to 2 hours. Makes 6 to 8 servings.

SALSA BEANS

2 (15½ ounce) cans great northern beans, rinsed, drained
2 (15 ounce) cans black beans, rinsed, drained
1 (15 ounce) can butter beans, rinsed, drained
1¼ cups barbecue sauce
¾ cup salsa
⅓ cup packed brown sugar

In slow cooker, combine all ingredients. Mix well. Cover. Cook on low 3 to 4 hours. Makes 8 servings.

NEW TWIST BAKE BEANS

3 slices bacon
½ cup chopped onion
½ cup ketchup
½ cup packed brown sugar
1 teaspoon mustard
1 (28 ounce) can pork and beans
¼ cup maple syrup

In slow cooker, combine all ingredients. Mix well. Cover. Cook on low 4 to 6 hours or high 2 to 3 hours. Makes 4 to 6 servings.

LASAGNA

1   (16 ounce) package wide egg noodles, cooked, drained
1   (16 ounce) carton cottage cheese
1   pound lean ground beef, cooked, drained
1   (26 ounce) jar spaghetti sauce
1   (16 ounce) package shredded mozzarella cheese

In slow cooker, layer 1/3 noodles. Place 1/3 cottage cheese. In skillet, combine beef with spaghetti sauce. Place 1/3 meat mixture over cottage cheese. Top with 1/3 cheese. Repeat process two more times. Cover. Cook on low 4 to 5 hours. Makes 4 to 6 servings.

TERRIFIC TORTELLINI

1   pound mild Italian sausage, browned, drained
1   (15 ounce) jar marinara sauce
1   (14 1/2 ounce) can Italian stewed tomatoes, undrained
1   cup sliced mushrooms
1   (9 ounce) package tortellini, thawed if frozen
1   cup shredded mozzarella cheese

In slow cooker, combine sausage, marinara sauce, tomatoes, and mushrooms. Mix well. Cover. Cook on low 7 to 8 hours. Add tortellini. Mix well. Top with cheese. Cover. Cook an additional 20 minutes. Makes 6 to 8 servings.

GREEK PASTA

- 2 pounds beef stew meat
- 1 cup sliced onion
- 1 (6 ounce) jar pitted Greek olives, drained
- 3/4 cup sun-dried tomatoes, chopped
- 1 (28 ounce) jar marinara sauce
- 6 cups hot cooked pasta

In slow cooker, place beef. Top with onion, olives, and tomatoes. Pour sauce over ingredients. Cover. Cook on low 8 to 10 hours. Serve with pasta. Makes 6 servings.

PIZZA CHICKEN PASTA

- 1 (16 ounce) package bow tie pasta, cooked
- 1 (26 ounce) jar spaghetti sauce
- 1 teaspoon pizza seasoning
- 3 skinless, boneless chicken breasts, cut into cubes
- 2 cups shredded mozzarella cheese

In slow cooker, combine all ingredients, except cheese. Cover. Cook on low 6 to 8 hours. Sprinkle cheese over top. Cover. Let set 10 minutes. Makes 4 to 6 servings.

MEAT LOVERS PIZZA PASTA

- 1 pound corkscrew pasta, cooked
- 1½ pounds lean ground beef, cooked, drained
- 1 pound Italian sausage, cooked, drained
- 2 (3 ounce) packages sliced pepperoni
- 4 (14 ounce) jars pizza sauce
- 2 (16 ounce) packages shredded mozzarella cheese
- ½ cup chopped green bell pepper
- ½ cup chopped onion

In slow cooker, combine all ingredients. Mix well. Cover. Cook on low 4 to 6 hours or high 2 hours. Makes 6 to 8 servings.

PIZZA TASTING PASTA

- 1 pound ground beef, browned, drained
- 1 small onion, chopped
- 2 (14 ounce) jars pizza sauce
- 1 (8 ounce) package pepperoni slices
- 2 cups macaroni, cooked, drained

In slow cooker, combine all ingredients. Mix well. Cover. Cook on low 3 to 4 hours. Makes 6 servings.

SPINACH & CHICKEN PASTA

2 cups cooked egg noodles
1 (10 ounce) package frozen chopped spinach, thawed, drained
2 tablespoons butter or margarine, melted
1½ cups diced cooked chicken
1 cup chicken gravy
1 (4 ounce) package cream cheese with chive and onion, softened
2 tablespoons grated Parmesan cheese

In slow cooker, place noodles. Spread spinach over noodles. Drizzle butter over spinach. In medium bowl, combine chicken, gravy, and cream cheese. Mix well. Pour mixture over spinach. Sprinkle cheese on top of mixture. Cover. Cook on low 3 to 4 hours. Makes 6 servings.

NACHO PASTA

1 (7 ounce) package macaroni, cooked, drained
1 (15 ounce) can black beans, rinsed, drained
1 (10¾ ounce) can nacho cheese soup
1/3 cup evaporated milk
1/2 cup crushed tortilla chips
1/2 cup shredded cheddar cheese

In slow cooker, combine macaroni, beans, soup, and milk. Mix well. Cover. Cook on low 3 to 4 hours. Stir. Top with chips and cheese. Cover. Cook an additional 20 minutes. Makes 4 to 6 servings.

CHEESE PASTA BAKE

4 cups cooked corkscrew pasta
1 (10¾ ounce) can cream of mushroom soup
1 (8 ounce) package shredded two cheese blend
½ cup grated Parmesan cheese
1 cup milk

In slow cooker, combine all ingredients. Mix well. Cover. Cook on low 3 to 4 hours. Makes 4 to 6 servings.

BEEF & MAC

1 pound lean ground beef
1 small onion, chopped
1 (10¾ ounce) can tomato soup
¼ cup water
1 tablespoon Worcestershire sauce
1 cup shredded cheddar cheese
3 cups cooked macaroni

In medium skillet, brown beef and onion over medium heat. Drain. In slow cooker, place beef mixture, soup, water, Worcestershire sauce, cheese, and macaroni. Mix well. Cover. Cook on low 3 to 4 hours. Makes 4 to 6 servings.

SAUCY RAVIOLI WITH MEATBALLS

2 (26 ounce) jars pasta sauce with mushrooms and onions
2 (24 ounce) packages frozen ravioli
1 (12 ounce) package frozen cooked Italian meatballs, thawed
1 (8 ounce) package shredded mozzarella cheese
½ cup finely shredded Parmesan cheese

Lightly coat inside slow cooker with nonstick cooking spray. Add 1 cup of the pasta sauce. Add frozen ravioli from one package and all of the meatballs. Sprinkle with 1 cup of the mozzarella cheese. Top with remaining pasta sauce from first jar. Add ravioli from remaining package and remaining 1 cup mozzarella cheese. Pour spaghetti sauce from second jar over mixture in cooker. Cover. Cook on low 4½ to 5 hours or high 2½ to 3 hours. Turn off cooker. Sprinkle ravioli mixture with Parmesan cheese. Cover. Let set for 15 minutes before serving. Makes 10 to 12 servings.

Better Homes and Gardens®
Test Kitchen

IS IT GOULASH

1 pound lean ground beef, browned, drained
4 cups cooked macaroni
1 (15 ounce) can chopped tomatoes
1 cup tomato sauce
1 teaspoon salt

In slow cooker, combine all ingredients.
Mix well. Cover. Cook on low 2½ to 3 hours.
Makes 4 servings.

BEST BOW TIE PASTA

1 (8 ounce) package bow tie pasta,
  cooked, drained
1 (16 ounce) jar spaghetti sauce with meat
1 (⅞ ounce) package Italian salad
  dressing mix
1 (8 ounce) package shredded mozzarella
  cheese

In slow cooker, combine pasta, sauce, and dressing
mix. Mix well. Cover. Cook on low 3 to 4 hours.
Sprinkle cheese over pasta during last 20 minutes
of cooking. Cover. Cook an additional 20 minutes
or until cheese melts. Makes 6 to 8 servings.

BOW TIE PASTA

1 pound Italian sausage links, sliced into 1-inch pieces
2 red bell peppers, chopped
1/2 cup vegetable broth
1/2 teaspoon Italian seasoning
8 ounces bow tie pasta, cooked

In slow cooker, combine sausage, peppers, broth, and seasoning. Mix well. Cover. Cook on low 4 to 6 hours. Add cooked pasta. Mix well. Makes 4 servings.

CHICKEN 'N NOODLES

2 1/2 to 3 1/2 pounds broiler chicken
2 cups water
1 teaspoon salt
1 cup chicken broth
2 tablespoons butter or margarine
1 (8 ounce) package egg noodles, cooked

In slow cooker, place chicken. Add remaining ingredients, except noodles. Cover. Cook on low 8 to 10 hours or high 4 to 5 hours. Remove chicken. Slice into chunks. Add chicken and noodles to slow cooker. Mix well. Cover. Cook on low an additional 1 hour. Makes 6 to 8 servings.

CHICKEN NOODLE CASSEROLE

1   (8 ounce) package noodles, cooked
4   cups chopped cooked chicken
2   (10³/₄ ounce) cans cream of chicken soup
1   cup milk
1   cup shredded cheddar cheese

In slow cooker, combine all ingredients. Mix well.
Cover. Cook on low 3 to 4 hours. Makes 6 servings.

GREEN CHILE CHICKEN ALFREDO

1¹/₄   pounds chicken breast, cut into bite-sized pieces
1   (16 ounce) jar Alfredo sauce
2   (4¹/₂ ounce) cans chopped green chiles
2   cups shredded mozzarella cheese
1   (10 ounce) package rigatoni noodles, cooked, warm

In slow cooker, place chicken. Pour Alfredo sauce
over chicken. Top with green chiles. Cover. Cook
on low 4 to 6 hours. Add rigatoni noodles to slow
cooker. Mix well. Sprinkle cheese over top. Cover.
Cook on high an additional 25 minutes. Makes 6
servings.

CHICKEN AND BROCCOLI ALFREDO

1¼ pounds chicken, cut into bite-sized pieces
1   (4½ ounce) can sliced mushrooms, drained
1   (16 ounce) jar Alfredo sauce
3   cups frozen broccoli, thawed
1   (10 ounce) package fettuccine noodles,
    cooked, warm

In slow cooker, place chicken and mushrooms.
Pour Alfredo sauce over top. Cover. Cook on
low 4 to 6 hours. Add broccoli. Mix well. Cover.
Cook on high an additional 20 minutes. Add
noodles. Mix well. Makes 5 servings.

FETTUCCINE NOODLES

2   (12 ounce) packages fettuccine noodles,
    cooked, drained
1   cup grated Parmesan cheese
¾   cup half-and-half
3½ tablespoons butter or margarine
3   tablespoons parsley

In slow cooker, combine all ingredients. Mix well.
Cover. Cook on low 2 to 3 hours or high 1½ hours.
Makes 6 to 8 servings.

CORNED BEEF PASTA

1   (7 ounce) package small shell pasta, cooked, drained
1   (12 ounce) can cooked corned beef
1   (10¾ ounce) can cream of chicken soup
1   (8 ounce) package cubed cheddar cheese
1   cup evaporated milk
½   cup diced onion

In slow cooker, combine all ingredients. Mix well. Cover. Cook on low 4 to 6 hours. Makes 4 servings.

CHILI SPAGHETTI

1   pound lean ground beef, browned, drained
1   medium onion, chopped
1   (15 ounce) can spicy chili beans
1   (14½ ounce) can tomatoes with green chiles
1   (8 ounce) can tomato sauce
½   teaspoon cumin

In slow cooker, combine all ingredients. Mix well. Cover. Cook on low 4 to 6 hours or high 1½ to 2 hours. Serve over cooked spaghetti. Makes 4 servings.

IMITATION CRAB PASTA

- 1 (8 ounce) package spiral pasta, cooked, drained
- 2 (8 ounce) packages imitation crabmeat, chopped
- 8 ounces shredded Velveeta® cheese
- 1 onion, chopped
- 2 cups sliced fresh mushrooms
- 1/2 cup chopped green bell pepper
- 1 1/2 teaspoon garlic salt

In slow cooker, place pasta, crabmeat, and cheese. In large skillet, sauté onions, mushrooms, green pepper, and garlic in butter until lightly golden. Pour mixture into slow cooker. Mix well. Cover. Cook on low 4 to 6 hours. Makes 4 to 6 servings.

PASTA & SMOKED SAUSAGE

- 1 (16 ounce) package smoked sausage, sliced 1/4 inch thick
- 2 (10 3/4 ounce) cans cream of mushroom soup
- 2 cups milk
- 6 cups cooked penne pasta
- 1 1/2 cups mozzarella cheese
- 2 cups frozen peas, thawed

In slow cooker, combine all ingredients. Mix well. Cover. Cook on low 4 to 6 hours or high 1 1/2 to 2 hours. Makes 6 servings.

WHAT'S COOKIN MACARONI

1 pound ground beef, browned, drained
1 small onion, sliced
2 tablespoons diced green bell pepper
4 cups slightly cooked macaroni
1 (10 ounce) can tomato sauce
1 cup shredded American cheese

In slow cooker, combine all ingredients.
Mix well. Cover. Cook on low 4 to 6 hours.
Makes 6 to 8 servings.

MAC 'N CHEESE FOR LUNCH

4 cups hot cooked macaroni
1 cup milk
2 (10¾ ounce) cans cheese soup
4 hot dogs, sliced
1 tablespoon butter

In slow cooker, combine all ingredients.
Mix well. Cover. Cook on low 3 to 4 hours.
Makes 4 to 6 servings.

HOT DOG MACARONI

3½   cups cooked macaroni
5   hot dogs, sliced
2   cups frozen peas
1½   cups milk
1   tablespoon butter or margarine
3   cups shredded cheddar cheese

In slow cooker, combine all ingredients. Mix well. Cover. Cook on low 3 to 4 hours. Makes 4 servings.

MACARONI & CHEESE

1   (8 ounce) package macaroni, cooked, drained
¼   cup butter, melted
1   (12 ounce) can evaporated milk
1   cup milk
½   teaspoon salt
3½   cups shredded American cheese

Coat inside of slow cooker with nonstick cooking spray. In large bowl, combine all ingredients. Mix well. Pour mixture into slow cooker. Cover. Cook on low 3 to 4 hours. Makes 4 to 6 servings.

JUST MAC & CHEESE

1 ($10^3/4$ ounce) can cheddar cheese soup
1 cup milk
4 cups cooked medium shell macaroni
1 cup shredded cheddar cheese
1 tablespoon butter

In slow cooker, combine all ingredients. Mix well.
Cover. Cook on low 3 to 4 hours or high $1^1/2$ to 2
hours. Makes 5 servings.

RAVIOLI LASAGNA

1 (28 ounce) jar pasta sauce
1 (25 ounce) package frozen cheese ravioli,
  partially thawed
1 (16 ounce) carton small curd cottage
  cheese
1 (16 ounce) package shredded mozzarella
  cheese
1/4 cup grated Parmesan cheese

In slow cooker, pour 1/2 pasta sauce and 1/2 ravioli.
Mix well. Spread 1/2 cottage cheese. Sprinkle 1/2
mozzarella over cottage cheese. In small bowl,
combine remaining sauce and ravioli. Mix well.
Pour over mozzarella. Spread remaining cottage
cheese. Sprinkle with remaining mozzarella cheese
and Parmesan cheese. Cover. Cook on low 4 to 6
hours. Makes 6 to 8 servings.

RANCH RAVIOLI

1   (25 ounce) package frozen chicken ravioli
1   cup roasted red peppers, rinsed, drained,
    chopped
3   cups ranch dressing
½   cup grated Parmesan cheese

In slow cooker, combine all ingredients. Cover.
Cook on low 4 to 6 hours. Makes 6 servings.

ALMOST BAKED RAVIOLI

1   (28 ounce) jar spaghetti sauce
1   (10¾ ounce) can cheddar cheese soup
1   (25 ounce) package frozen sausage ravioli
1½   cups shredded mozzarella cheese

Coat inside of slow cooker with nonstick cooking
spray. In slow cooker, combine all ingredients,
except cheese. Mix well. Cover. Cook on low 4 to 6
hours or high 1½ to 2 hours. Sprinkle cheese over
mixture. Makes 4 to 6 servings.

RAVE ABOUT RAVIOLI

- 1 tablespoon olive oil
- 1/2 cup chopped onion
- 1 clove garlic, minced
- 2 (26 ounce) jars four cheese flavored tomato pasta sauce
- 2 (25 ounce) packages frozen beef ravioli
- 2 cups shredded mozzarella cheese, divided

In large skillet over medium high heat, sauté onion and garlic in oil until golden brown. Add pasta sauce. Mix well. In slow cooker, place 1 cup of sauce mixture. Add 1 package ravioli. Top with 1 cup cheese. Add remaining package of ravioli. Top with remaining cheese. Pour remaining sauce over top. Cover. Cook on low for 5 to 6 hours. Makes 8 to 10 servings.

MEXICAN PASTA SAUCE

- 2 (12 ounce) packages mild Mexican cheese
- 4 tablespoons milk
- 2 cups chopped plum tomatoes
  Favorite pasta

In slow cooker, combine cheese and milk. Cover. Cook on low 2 hours or until cheese has melted. Add tomatoes. Mix well. Pour mixture over favorite pasta. Makes 6 to 8 servings.

PIZZA SAUCE FOR PASTA

2 (14 ounce) jars pizza sauce
2 cups chopped tomatoes
1 cup diced pepperoni
1/2 cup sliced green onion

In slow cooker, combine all ingredients. Mix well. Cover. Cook on low 3 to 4 hours or high 1½ to 2 hours. Serve over hot pasta. Makes 6 to 8 servings.

SPAGHETTI SAUCE

1 pound Italian sausage, browned, drained
1 (28 ounce) jar spaghetti sauce
1/2 cup chopped onion
1 clove garlic, minced
1 cup chopped tomatoes
1 teaspoon sugar

In slow cooker, combine all ingredients. Mix well. Cover. Cook on low 3 to 4 hours or high 1½ to 2 hours. Makes 4 servings.

SAUSAGE TOPPER FOR FETTUCCINI

1 pound fully cooked polish sausage, cut into 1/2-inch pieces
2 (15 ounce) cans chunky garlic and herb tomato sauce
1 (16 ounce) package frozen stir-fry bell peppers and onions, thawed

In slow cooker, combine all ingredients. Mix well. Cover. Cook on low 3 to 4 hours. Serve mixture over cooked fettuccine. Makes 4 servings.

DON'T PASS UP TOPPER

2 pounds ground beef, browned, drained
1 1/2 cups chopped onion
1 (12 ounce) can beer
2 1/2 tablespoons chili powder
1 (15 ounce) can tomato sauce
2 cups ketchup
1/4 cup mustard

In slow cooker, combine all ingredients. Mix well. Cover. Cook on low 3 to 4 hours. Serve over spaghetti. Makes 6 to 8 servings.

QUICK BEEF TOPPER

2   pounds beef, cubed
2   (10¾ ounce) cans cream of mushroom soup
1   (4 ounce) can mushrooms, with liquid
½   cup wine

In slow cooker, combine all ingredients. Cover.
Cook on low 6 to 8 hours. Serve over rice or
noodles. Makes 4 to 6 servings.

BEEF STROGANOFF

1   pound beef stew meat, cut into 1-inch cubes
1   medium onion, chopped
2   cups sliced mushrooms
1   (14½ ounce) can beef broth
1   (8 ounce) container cream cheese with
    chive and onion

In slow cooker, place meat, onion, mushrooms,
and broth. Cover. Cook on low 6 to 8 hours or
high 3 to 4 hours. Add cream cheese before serving.
Stir well. Serve over noodles. Makes 4 servings.

OUT ALL DAY BEEF STROGANOFF

4 pounds stewing beef, cut into 1-inch cubes
2 (10¾ ounce) cans cream of mushroom soup
1 (1 ounce) package dry onion soup mix
1 (8 ounce) container sour cream

In slow cooker, combine all ingredients, except sour cream. Cover. Cook on low 8 hours. Add sour cream. Mix well. Serve over noodles. Makes 6 to 8 servings.

SHORT STEPS STROGANOFF

2 pounds lean ground beef, browned, drained
2 (10¾ ounce) cans cream of mushroom soup
1/3 cup evaporated milk
1/4 cup ketchup
1/2 cup sour cream

In slow cooker, combine all ingredients, except sour cream. Mix well. Cook on low 4 to 6 hours. Add sour cream. Mix well. Serve over noodles.
Makes 4 to 6 servings.

CHICKEN STROGANOFF

2 pounds skinless, boneless chicken breast halves and/or thighs, cut into 1-inch pieces
1 cup chopped onion
1 (4 ounce) can sliced mushrooms, drained
2 (10¾ ounce) cans cream of mushroom soup with roasted garlic
⅓ cup water
12 ounces dried wide egg noodles
1 (8 ounce) carton dairy sour cream
Freshly ground black pepper
Fresh thyme sprigs

In slow cooker, combine chicken pieces, onion, and mushrooms. In medium bowl, stir together cream of mushroom soup and water. Pour over chicken and vegetables. Cover and cook on low 6 to 7 hours or high 3 to 3½ hours. Cook noodles according to package directions; drain well. Just before serving, stir sour cream into mixture in slow cooker. Serve over hot cooked noodles. Sprinkle with pepper and garnish with thyme. Makes 6 to 8 servings.

Better Homes and Gardens
Test Kitchen

STEAK CASSEROLE

2 pounds round steak, cut into bite-sized pieces
4 potatoes, peeled, diced
1 onion, thinly sliced
1 (16 ounce) can French cut green beans, drained
1 (10¾ ounce) can tomato soup
1 (14½ ounce) can stewed tomatoes, drained

In slow cooker, layer steak, potatoes, onion, green beans, soup, and tomatoes. Cover. Cook on low 8 hours. Makes 6 to 8 servings.

SOUPED UP BEEF CASSEROLE

2 pounds stew beef, cut into bite-sized pieces
1 (10¾ ounce) can cream of mushroom soup
1 (4 ounce) can sliced mushrooms, drained
1 (1⅜ ounce) package dry onion soup mix
½ cup beef broth

In slow cooker, combine all ingredients. Mix well. Cover. Cook on low 8 to 10 hours or high 4 to 5 hours. Makes 6 to 8 servings.

POTATOES & SAUSAGE CASSEROLE

8 to 10 large potatoes, peeled, sliced
1 pound sausage links
2½ cups shredded cheddar cheese
1 (10¾ ounce) can cream of mushroom soup
1 cup milk

In slow cooker, combine all ingredients. Mix well.
Cover. Cook on low 8 to 10 hours. Makes 8 servings.

NOT JUST BEANS 'N WIENERS

1 pound wieners, cut in fourths
3 (15 ounce) cans pork and beans
½ cup ketchup
½ cup diced onion
¼ cup molasses
1 teaspoon mustard

In slow cooker, combine all ingredients. Mix well.
Cover. Cook on low 4 to 6 hours. Makes 8 servings.

ALOHA BEANIE WIENIE CASSEROLE

2 (16 ounce) packages hot dogs, cut into pieces
2 (16 ounce) cans baked beans
2 (8 ounce) cans pineapple chunks, drained
1/2 cup packed brown sugar

In slow cooker, combine all ingredients. Cover. Cook on low 3 to 4 hours. Makes 6 to 8 servings.

BEANIE WIENIE CASSEROLE

2 (16 ounce) cans baked beans
1 (16 ounce) package hot dogs, cut into pieces
1 cup barbecue sauce
1/4 cup packed brown sugar

In slow cooker, combine all ingredients. Cover. Cook on low 2 to 3 hours. Makes 4 servings.

PORK & VEGGIE SUPPER

4   boneless pork loin chops, cubed, browned
2   (12 ounce) jars pork gravy
3   tablespoons ketchup
2   cups chopped potatoes
2   cups mixed vegetables

In slow cooker, combine all ingredients. Mix well.
Cover. Cook on low 8 to 9 hours. Makes 6 servings.

ROLLED UP ENCHILADAS

2   pounds ground beef, browned, drained
2   (17½ ounce) jars enchilada sauce
4   cups shredded cheddar cheese
8   flour tortillas

In slow cooker, combine all ingredients, except
tortillas. Cover. Cook on low 2½ to 3 hours. Spoon
2 tablespoons of mixture on each tortilla. Roll up
and place seam side down in baking dish. Top with
remaining mixture. Bake at 350 degrees for 20
minutes. Makes 8 servings.

ENCHILADA CASSEROLE

- 2 (10¾ ounce) cans creamy ranchero soup
- 1 cup water
- 3 cups cubed cooked chicken
- 5 flour tortillas, cut into strips
- 1 cup shredded cheddar cheese

In slow cooker, combine all ingredients, except cheese. Mix well. Cover. Cook on low 4 to 6 hours. Add cheese during last 15 minutes of cooking. Makes 6 to 8 servings.

TACO CASSEROLE

- 1 pound lean ground beef
- 1 cup salsa
- 1 teaspoon chili powder
- 2 cups crushed tortilla chips, divided
- 1 cup Mexican-style cheese
- 2 cups shredded lettuce
- 1 tomato, chopped

In large skillet, brown beef over medium heat. Drain. Add salsa and chili powder. Mix well. In slow cooker, place half of meat mixture. Layer 1 cup chips and ½ cup cheese. Place remaining beef mixture over cheese. Layer remaining chips and cheese. Cover. Cook on low 3 to 4 hours. Serve with lettuce and tomato. Makes 6 servings.

LAYERED MEXICAN CASSEROLE

1 pound lean ground beef
1 medium onion, chopped
1 (10¾ ounce) can cream of mushroom soup
1 (11 ounce) can Mexican-style whole kernel corn, drained
1 (10½ ounce) package corn chips, crushed
1 (10 ounce) can enchilada sauce
2 cups shredded Mexican-style cheese

In large skillet, brown beef and onion over medium heat. Drain. In slow cooker, add beef mixture, soup, and corn. Mix well. Layer with corn chips then enchilada sauce. Cover. Cook on low 3 to 4 hours. Add cheese. Cover. Cook an additional 20 minutes. Makes 6 servings.

MEXICAN CASSEROLE

6 corn tortillas, cut in strips
1 pound lean ground beef, browned, drained
1 (10¾ ounce) can cream of mushroom soup
1 (10¾ ounce) can cream of chicken soup
1 (14½ ounce) can chopped tomatoes with green chiles
8 ounces Velveeta® cheese, cubed

In slow cooker, place tortilla strips. Layer beef, soup, and tomatoes over tortilla strips. Top with cheese. Cover. Cook on low 3 to 4 hours.

CHILI & TAMALE CASSEROLE

- 2 (14 ounce) cans chili con carne
- 6 tamales
- 1/2 cup chopped onion
- 2 cups crushed corn chips
- 1 cup shredded cheddar cheese

In slow cooker, cover bottom with chili. Add tamales, onion, chips, and cheese. Cover. Cook on low 4 to 6 hours or high 1½ to 2 hours. Makes 4 to 6 servings.

SOUTHWEST TACO PIE

- 1 pound ground beef, browned, drained
- 1 (10¾ ounce) can tomato soup
- 1 cup salsa
- 1/2 cup milk
- 8 corn tortillas, cut into 1-inch pieces
- 1½ cups shredded cheddar cheese

In slow cooker, combine all ingredients. Mix well. Cover. Cook on low 4 to 6 hours or high 1½ to 2 hours. Makes 4 servings.

CABBAGE WITH BEEF

1 pound lean ground beef, browned, drained
5 cups shredded cabbage
1 cup shredded carrots
1/4 cup beef broth
1/2 cup tomato sauce
  Salt and pepper

In slow cooker, combine all ingredients. Mix well.
Cover. Cook on low 4 to 6 hours or high 1½ to
2 hours. Makes 4 to 6 servings.

ON THE RUN TUNA CASSEROLE

2 (10¾ ounce) cans cream of mushroom soup
1 cup milk
3 (6 ounce) cans water-packed tuna, drained
4 cups hot cooked medium noodles
2 tablespoons butter

In slow cooker, combine all ingredients. Cover.
Cook on low 4 to 6 hours or high 1½ to 2 hours.
Makes 6 to 8 servings.

POTLUCK TATER CASSEROLE

1	(32 ounce) bag frozen tater tots
1	pound ground beef, browned, drained
1/2	teaspoon salt
2	(14 1/2 ounce) cans green beans, drained
1	(10 3/4 ounce) can cream of mushroom soup
1/4	cup milk

In slow cooker, cover bottom with tater tots.
In medium bowl, combine beef, salt, green beans,
mushroom soup, and milk. Mix well. Pour over tater
tots. Cover. Cook on low 4 to 6 hours or high
3 hours. Makes 6 to 8 servings.

MEATBALL & HASH BROWN CASSEROLE

1	(30 ounce) package frozen shredded hash brown potatoes, thawed
1	(10 3/4 ounce) can cream of chicken soup
1	cup shredded cheddar cheese
1	cup sour cream
1	onion, chopped
20	premade fully cooked meatballs

In slow cooker, combine hash browns, soup,
cheese, sour cream, and onion. Mix well.
Top with meatballs. Cover. Cook on low 6 to
8 hours. Makes 8 servings.

LAYERED CASSEROLE

2 pounds potatoes, sliced thin
3 stalks celery, diced
2 cloves garlic, minced
1 green bell pepper, diced
1 onion, diced
1 pound smoked sausage, sliced

In slow cooker, place potato slices. In large bowl, combine garlic, bell pepper, onion, and celery. Add half of mixture to slow cooker. Add half of sausage over vegetables. Add remaining vegetables. Add remaining sausage. Cover. Cook on low 10 to 12 hours. Makes 8 servings.

CABBAGE & CORNED BEEF CASSEROLE

1 medium head cabbage, shredded
3/4 pound corned beef, cubed
1 small onion, chopped
1 (15½ ounce) can white hominy, drained
1 cup water
1/4 teaspoon hot pepper sauce

In slow cooker, combine all ingredients. Mix well. Cover. Cook on low 4 to 6 hours. Makes 6 servings.

TUNA CASSEROLE

7 ounces wide egg noodles, cooked
1 (10¾ ounce) can cream of mushroom soup
1 (12 ounce) can evaporated milk
2 (6 ounce) cans water-packed tuna, drained
1½ cups frozen sweet peas
1 tablespoon minced onion
1 (2.8 ounce) can French fried onions

In slow cooker, combine all ingredients, except French fried onions. Mix well. Cover. Cook on low 4 to 5 hours. Top with French fried onions before serving. Makes 6 servings.

KIDS LOVE IT CHEESEBURGER CASSEROLE

2 pounds lean ground beef, browned, drained
2 (10¾ ounce) cans cheddar cheese soup
1 (20 ounce) package frozen crinkle-cut French fries

In slow cooker, combine beef and soup. Mix well. Top with French fries. Cover. Cook on low 6 to 8 hours. Makes 6 to 8 servings.

SAUSAGE AND HASH BROWN CASSEROLE

1½   pounds Polish sausage, sliced
1   (16 ounce) package frozen hash brown
     potatoes
1   (10¾ ounce) can cheddar cheese soup
1   cup evaporated milk
1   green bell pepper, diced
1   bunch green onions, diced

Coat inside of slow cooker with nonstick cooking
spray. In slow cooker, place all ingredients.
Mix well. Cover. Cook on low 4 to 6 hours. Makes
6 servings.

BACON POTATO CASSEROLE

2   eggs
2   tablespoons flour
½   cup evaporated milk
1   pound bacon, cooked, crumbled
1   (16 ounce) package hash brown potatoes
1   small onion, diced
2   cups shredded cheddar cheese

Coat inside of slow cooker with nonstick cooking
spray. In small bowl, combine eggs, flour, and
milk. Mix well. In slow cooker, combine all
ingredients. Mix well. Cover. Cook on low 4 to 6
hours. Makes 6 servings.

ITALIAN SAUSAGE POTATO CASSEROLE

1 pound Italian sausage, browned, drained
1 (16 ounce) package hash brown potatoes
  with peppers and onions
2 cups shredded cheddar cheese
1 teaspoon salt
1/2 teaspoon pepper

Coat inside of slow cooker with nonstick cooking
spray. In slow cooker, combine all ingredients.
Cover. Cook on low 4 to 6 hours. Makes 6 servings.

COWBOY CHILI CASSEROLE

1 (40 ounce) can chili with beans
1 (8 ounce) package shredded cheddar cheese
2 cups crushed nacho cheese flavored
  tortilla chips
1 (4 ounce) can chopped green chiles
1 (2¼ ounce) can sliced black olives,
  drained

In slow cooker, combine all ingredients. Cover.
Cook on low 4 to 6 hours. Makes 6 servings.

ONE DISH CHICKEN CASSEROLE

    2   (10¾ ounce) cans cream of mushroom soup
    2   cups water
    ¾   cup uncooked white rice
    ½   teaspoon paprika
    4   skinless, boneless chicken breast halves

In slow cooker, combine soup, water, rice, and
paprika. Mix well. Place chicken on mixture.
Cover. Cook on low 8 to 10 hours or high 4 to
6 hours. Makes 4 servings.

STIR FRY CHICKEN CASSEROLE

    2   cups uncooked instant rice
    1   (8 ounce) can sliced water chestnuts,
        drained
    2   cups cooked chicken
    1   (16 ounce) package frozen stir-fry
        vegetables, thawed
    1   (14½ ounce) can chicken broth
    ¼   cup soy sauce
    ½   teaspoon garlic powder
    ½   teaspoon ground ginger

In slow cooker, layer rice, chestnuts, chicken, and
vegetables. In small bowl combine broth, soy sauce,
garlic, and ginger. Mix well. Pour over vegetables.
Cover. Cook on low 6 to 8 hours. Makes 4 servings.

ONE FOR ALL CHICKEN DINNER

3 pounds whole chicken, cut up
4 carrots, peeled, sliced
4 potatoes, peeled, sliced
2 celery stalks, sliced
1 cup Italian dressing
1/2 cup chicken broth

In slow cooker, place chicken. Add carrots, potatoes, and celery. Pour dressing and broth over vegetables. Cover. Cook on low 8 to 10 hours. Makes 6 servings.

PLAY 'N EAT CHICKEN DINNER

4 skinless, boneless chicken breasts
1 (10$\frac{3}{4}$ ounce) can cream of chicken soup
1/3 cup milk
1 (6 ounce) package stuffing mix
1$\frac{2}{3}$ cups hot water

In slow cooker, place chicken. In small bowl, combine soup and milk. Mix well. Pour mixture over chicken. In medium bowl, combine stuffing and water. Spoon stuffing over chicken. Cover. Cook on low 6 to 8 hours. Makes 4 servings.

CHICKEN & DROP DUMPLINGS

```
3   pounds skinless, boneless chicken thighs,
    cut into bite-sized pieces
3   (14 ounce) cans chicken broth
1   pound small red potatoes, cubed
2   cups sliced carrots
1   onion, chopped
2   cups Bisquick®
½   cup water
```

In slow cooker, combine chicken, broth, potatoes, carrots, and onion. Cover. Cook on low 9 to 10 hours. In small bowl, combine Bisquick and water. Mix well. Drop dough into chicken mixture. Cover. Cook on high an additional 45 to 55 minutes or until dumplings are dry in center. Makes 5 servings.

EASY SUPPER

```
2   pounds lean ground beef, browned, drained
3   stalks celery, chopped
½   green bell pepper, chopped
1   small onion, chopped
1   teaspoon sugar
½   teaspoon salt
1   (10¾ ounce) can cream of mushroom soup
```

In slow cooker, combine all ingredients. Cover. Cook on low 4 to 6 hours. Serve over biscuits or with cheddar cheese. Makes 6 to 8 servings.

AMAZING ASPARAGUS & CHICKEN CASSEROLE

- 2 cups cooked cubed chicken
- 1 (8 ounce) package frozen chopped asparagus, thawed
- 1 (10¾ ounce) can cream of chicken soup
- 1 (2.8 ounce) can French fried onions
- ¼ cup water

In slow cooker, combine all ingredients. Mix well. Cover. Cook on low 4 to 6 hours. Makes 4 servings.

JUST AHEAD POTATOES & BEEF

- 1 (17 ounce) package fully cooked beef tips with gravy
- 2 cups frozen chunky-style hash brown potatoes
- 1 red bell pepper, cut in 1-inch strips
- 1 green bell pepper, cut in 1-inch strips
- 1 small onion, cut in wedges
- ½ cup water

In slow cooker, combine all ingredients. Cover. Cook on low 4 to 6 hours. Makes 4 servings.

TUNA & SPINACH CASSEROLE

- 2 (10 ounce) packages frozen chopped spinach, thawed, drained
- 2 (6 ounce) cans water-packed tuna, drained
- 1 cup crushed seasoned bread crumbs
- 1 cup mayonnaise
- 1/2 cup sour cream
- 1 teaspoon lemon juice
- 1/4 cup Parmesan cheese

In slow cooker, combine all ingredients, except cheese. Mix well. Cover. Cook on low 4 to 6 hours. Add cheese. Cover. Cook an additional 20 minutes. Makes 4 servings.

CHEESY TUNA CASSEROLE

- 2 (7.25 ounce) boxes macaroni and cheese
- 1 tablespoon butter
- 1 (15 ounce) can peas, drained
- 3 (6 ounce) cans water-packed tuna, drained
- 1 cup shredded American cheese

Prepare macaroni and cheese according to package directions. In slow cooker combine macaroni mixture and remaining ingredients. Mix well. Cover. Cook on low 4 to 6 hours or high 2 to 3 hours. Makes 6 servings.

BEEF & TATER-TOTS CASSEROLE

1½ pounds ground beef, browned, drained
1 (16 ounce) package frozen green beans
1 cup shredded American cheese
1 (10¾ ounce) can cream of mushroom soup
1 (21 ounce) package frozen tater tots

In slow cooker, combine all ingredients, except tater tots. Mix well. Place tater tots on mixture. Cover. Cook on low 4 to 6 hours. Makes 6 servings.

ONE POT CHICKEN DINNER

6 skinless, boneless chicken breasts
2 (6 ounce) packages stuffing mix
½ cup chicken broth
1 (12 ounce) jar chicken gravy
2 (15 ounce) cans green beans, drained

In large skillet, brown chicken lightly. Place in slow cooker. In large bowl, combine stuffing, broth, and gravy. Mix well. Cover chicken with half of stuffing mixture. Spread green beans over stuffing. Top with rest of stuffing. Cover. Cook on low 6 to 8 hours. Makes 4 to 6 servings.

SHOESTRING CASSEROLE

2   (4 ounce) cans shoestring potatoes
2   (10¾ ounce) cans cream of mushroom soup
2   (6 ounce) cans water-packed tuna, drained
½   cup evaporated milk
1   (4½ ounce) jar sliced mushrooms, drained

In slow cooker, combine all ingredients.
Mix well. Cover. Cook on low 4 to 6 hours.
Makes 6 to 8 servings.

CARROT CASSEROLE

8   cups sliced carrots
1   onion, chopped
1   (10¾ ounce) can cream of mushroom soup
1   (4 ounce) can sliced mushrooms, drained
¼   cup evaporated milk
1   cup crushed butter-flavored crackers

In slow cooker, combine all ingredients, except
crackers. Mix well. Cover. Cook on low 8 to 10
hours. During last 30 minutes of cooking, stir
and sprinkle cracker crumbs over carrot mixture.
Cover. Cook remaining 30 minutes. Makes 8 servings.

KIND OF A HAM PASTA

2 cups cubed cooked ham
2 cups cooked macaroni noodles
1 (10¾ ounce) can cheddar cheese soup
1 cup frozen peas
1 cup crushed potato chips

In slow cooker, combine all ingredients, except chips. Mix well. Cover. Cook on low 3 to 4 hours. Stir and top with chips. Cover. Cook an additional 30 minutes. Makes 4 servings.

VEGGI & SAUSAGE CASSEROLE

2 medium potatoes, sliced
3 tablespoons Italian dressing
1 tablespoon Dijon mustard
2 onions, sliced
2 medium carrots, sliced
2 cups chopped cabbage
1 pound Polska Kielbasa, sliced
1 (14½ ounce) can Italian-style chopped tomatoes

In slow cooker, place potatoes. In small bowl, mix dressing and mustard. Drizzle one-third of dressing mixture over potatoes. Place onions and carrots over potatoes. Drizzle one-third of dressing over carrots. Place cabbage over carrots. Drizzle remaining dressing over cabbage. Top with sausage. Pour tomatoes over sausage. Cover. Cook on low 7 to 8 hours. Makes 4 to 6 servings.

CHICKEN & RICE DISH

- 3 pounds skinless, boneless chicken pieces, browned, cubed
- 1½ cups diced cooked ham
- 1 onion, chopped
- 1 red bell pepper, chopped
- 1 (14 ounce) can chicken broth
- 1 (8 ounce) package wild rice mix

In slow cooker, combine all ingredients. Mix well. Cover. Cook on low 8 to 10 hours. Makes 6 to 8 servings.

CHICKEN AND RICE

- 4 skinless, boneless chicken breasts, cut into bite-sized pieces
- 3 (10¾ ounce) cans cream of chicken soup
- 1 cup instant rice, uncooked

In slow cooker, place chicken. In small bowl, combine soup and rice. Pour over chicken. Cover. Cook over low heat 6 to 8 hours. Makes 4 servings.

RICE & SHRIMP DISH

3 boil-in-bags rice
2 (12 ounce) jars Alfredo sauce
2 (10 ounce) cans diced tomatoes with basil
2 pounds cooked shrimp
1 cup shredded Parmesan cheese

Prepare rice according to package directions. In slow cooker, combine Alfredo sauce and tomatoes. Cover. Cook on low 3 to 4 hours. Add shrimp. Pour mixture over rice. Sprinkle cheese over mixture. Makes 6 to 8 servings.

JUST SPAM IT RICE

2 (12 ounce) cans Spam®, cubed
1 medium onion, chopped
1 teaspoon butter
3 (15 ounce) cans green beans, drained
1½ cups tomato sauce
1 teaspoon garlic powder

In large skillet, brown Spam and onion in butter over medium high heat. In slow cooker, combine Spam mixture, green beans, tomato sauce, and garlic powder. Mix well. Cover. Cook on low 4 to 6 hours or high 1½ to 2 hours. Serve over cooked rice. Makes 6 to 8 servings.

CHICKEN AND SAUSAGE GUMBO

- 1/3 cup all-purpose flour
- 1/3 cup vegetable oil
- 3 cups water
- 12 ounces cooked smoked sausage links, quartered and sliced
- 1 1/2 cups chopped cooked chicken
- 2 cups sliced okra or 1 (10 ounce) package frozen okra, partially thawed and sliced 1/2 inch thick
- 1 large onion, chopped
- 1/2 cup chopped green pepper
- 1 rib celery, chopped
- 4 cloves garlic, minced
- 1/2 teaspoon salt
- 1/2 teaspoon black pepper
- 1/4 teaspoon cayenne pepper
- 3 cups hot cooked rice

In heavy saucepan, stir together flour and oil until smooth. Cook over medium-high heat for 5 minutes, stirring constantly. Reduce heat to medium. Cook and stir constantly about 15 minutes more or until a dark, reddish brown roux forms. Cool. Pour water into slow cooker. Stir in roux. Add sausage, chicken, okra, onion, green pepper, celery, garlic, salt, black pepper, and cayenne pepper. Cover. Cook on low 6 to 7 hours or high 3 to 3 1/2 hours. Skim off fat. Serve over hot cooked rice. Makes 5 servings.

Better Homes and Gardens®
Test Kitchen

BEAN-AND-RICE-STUFFED PEPPERS

4 medium green, red, and/or yellow sweet peppers
1 (15 ounce) can chili beans with chili gravy
1 cup cooked converted rice
1 cup shredded Monterey Jack cheese, divided
1 (15 ounce) can tomato sauce

Remove and reserve pepper tops. Remove membranes and seeds from peppers. In medium bowl, stir together chili beans, rice, and ½ cup of the cheese; spoon into peppers. Pour tomato sauce into slow cooker. Place peppers, filled sides up, in slow cooker. Place pepper tops beside peppers. Cover. Cook on low 6 to 6½ hours or on high 3 to 3½ hours. Transfer peppers to serving plate. Spoon tomato mixture from cooker over peppers. Sprinkle with remaining cheese. Replace pepper tops. Makes 4 servings.

Better Homes and Gardens®

Test Kitchen

BEEF MIXTURE ON RICE

2 pounds beef, cubed, browned
1 cup beef broth
1 small onion, chopped
2 (10¾ ounce) cans cream of mushroom soup
3 tablespoons dry onion soup mix

In slow cooker, combine all ingredients. Mix well. Cover. Cook on low 6 to 8 hours or high 2 to 3 hours. Serve over rice. Makes 6 to 8 servings.

CREAMY GREEN CHILE RICE

1½ cups uncooked instant rice
1 (10¾ ounce) can cream of celery soup
1½ cups evaporated milk
1 cup shredded cheddar cheese
1 (4 ounce) can chopped green chiles

In slow cooker, combine all ingredients.
Mix well. Cover. Cook on low 6 to 8 hours.
Makes 4 to 6 servings.

WILD RICE DISH

1 pound lean ground beef, browned, drained
1 (6.2 ounce) package fast-cooking wild rice mix, prepared
1 (10¾ ounce) can tomato soup
¼ cup evaporated milk
1 cup shredded cheddar cheese

In slow cooker, combine all ingredients, except
cheese. Mix well. Cover. Cook on low 4 hours.
Mix and top with cheese. Cover. Cook an additional
15 minutes. Makes 4 servings.

CHICKEN & WILD RICE

8	skinless, boneless chicken breast halves
1½	cups water
1	(6 ounce) package seasoned long grain wild rice mix
2	(10¾ ounce) cans cream of celery soup

In slow cooker, place chicken. In large bowl, combine remaining ingredients. Mix well. Pour mixture over chicken. Cover. Cook on low 8 to 10 hours. Makes 8 servings.

JAMBALAYA

1	small onion, chopped
⅓	cup diced green bell pepper
⅓	cup diced celery
1	cup chicken broth
1	(14½ ounce) can diced tomatoes
1	(16 ounce) package smoked sausage, cut into 1-inch slices
1	teaspoon Cajun seasoning
1	cup long grain rice, cooked

In slow cooker, combine all ingredients. Mix well. Cover. Cook on low 6 to 8 hours. Makes 4 servings.

EASY CHICKEN RAREBIT

- 1¾ pounds skinless, boneless chicken breast halves
- 1 (14 to 16 ounce) jar cheddar cheese pasta sauce
- 1 tablespoon Worcestershire sauce
- 1 large onion, halved crosswise and thinly sliced
- 6 pumpernickel or rye buns, split and toasted, or 6 slices pumpernickel or rye bread, toasted and halved diagonally
- 4 slices bacon, crisp-cooked, drained, and crumbled
- 1 tomato, chopped
  Kosher dill pickles

Cut chicken diagonally into ½-inch-thick slices; set aside. In slow cooker, stir together pasta sauce and Worcestershire sauce. Add onion and chicken slices. Cover and cook on low 4 to 5 hours or high 2 to 2½ hours. To serve, spoon chicken and sauce mixture over bun halves. Sprinkle with crumbled bacon and tomato. Serve with dill pickles. Makes 6 servings.

Better Homes and Gardens®
Test Kitchen

CHIPPED BEEF ON TOAST

2   (10¾ ounce) cans potato soup
1   tablespoon butter
¼   cup evaporated milk
2   cups jar chipped beef, rinsed, chopped

In slow cooker, combine all ingredients. Mix well.
Cover. Cook on low 2½ to 3 hours. Serve over
toast. Makes 4 servings.

AFTER THE GAME TACOS

2   pounds lean ground beef, browned, drained
½   cup chopped onion
2   (11¼ ounce) cans Fiesta® chili beef soup
½   cup water

In slow cooker, combine all ingredients. Mix well.
Cover. Cook on low 3 to 4 hours. Serve with cheese,
lettuce, tomatoes, sour cream, and taco shells.
Makes 10 to 15 servings.

EASY TO MAKE DRESSING

2   (6 ounce) packages stuffing mix
1   cup chicken broth
2   cups chicken gravy
1   cup diced onion
3/4 cup diced celery

In large bowl, combine all ingredients. Mix well.
Pour mixture in slow cooker. Cover. Cook on low
4 to 6 hours. Makes 6 to 8 servings.

NO BAKE DRESSING

15   cups dried bread crumbs
2   cups chopped celery
1   cup diced onion
1 1/2 cups chicken broth
1   (10 3/4 ounce) can cream of chicken soup
1/4 cup melted butter
2   teaspoons sage
1   teaspoon salt

Coat inside of slow cooker with nonstick cooking
spray. In slow cooker, combine all ingredients.
Mix well. Cook on low 4 to 6 hours. Makes 8 to
10 servings.

GAME TIME JOES

2   pounds lean ground beef
1   cup chopped onion
1/2 cup chopped green bell pepper
2   (14 ounce) jars pizza sauce
3/4 cup sliced pepperoni, chopped
1   cup shredded mozzarella cheese

In medium skillet, combine beef, onion, and pepper. Cook over medium heat until browned. Drain. Pour mixture into slow cooker. Add pizza sauce and pepperoni. Mix well. Cover. Cook on low 4 to 6 hours. Serve with cheese and hamburger buns. Makes 10 to 12 servings.

TURKEY SLOPPY JOES

2   pounds lean ground turkey, browned
2   small onions, chopped
2   (15 1/2 ounce) cans sloppy Joe sauce
4   cups corn

In slow cooker, combine all ingredients. Mix well. Cover. Cook on low 4 to 6 hours. Serve with hamburger buns. Makes 6 to 8 servings.

FIXIN BEEF BURGERS

2½ pounds ground beef, browned, drained
½ cup ketchup
¼ cup diced onion
2 (10¾ ounce) cans cream of mushroom soup
½ cup milk

In slow cooker, combine all ingredients. Cover. Cook on low 4 to 6 hours. Serve with hamburger buns. Makes 6 servings.

BBQ HAMBURGERS

2 pounds lean ground beef, browned, drained
1½ tablespoons brown sugar
1 cup tomato soup
½ cup ketchup
1 teaspoon dry mustard
¼ cup diced onion

In slow cooker, combine all ingredients. Mix well. Cover. Cook on low 4 to 6 hours or high 1½ to 3 hours. Serve with hamburger buns. Makes 6 to 8 servings.

BARBEQUE SANDWICHES

2 pounds lean ground beef, browned, drained
1/2 cup diced celery
1/3 cup diced green bell pepper
1/4 cup diced onion
1/2 cup barbecue sauce

In slow cooker, combine all ingredients. Cover.
Cook on low 4 to 6 hours or high 1½ to 2 hours.
Serve with hamburger buns. Makes 6 servings.

WAKE UP TO BREAKFAST

1½ cups oatmeal
3 cups water
2 cups sliced apples
1/2 teaspoon cinnamon

Coat inside of slow cooker with nonstick cooking
spray. In slow cooker, combine all ingredients.
Mix well. Cover. Cook on low 8 to 9 hours. Can add
1/2 cup raisins. Makes 4 to 6 servings.

Chicken Burritos, page 256

Honey-Mustard Barbecue Pork Ribs, page 230

BEEF, PORK, POULTRY, & SEAFOOD

POT ROAST DINNER

3	potatoes, sliced
3	carrots, sliced
1	small onion, sliced
1	teaspoon salt
3	to 4 pounds beef chuck roast
1/4	cup beef broth

In slow cooker, add all vegetables. Salt roast and place on vegetables. Pour broth over roast. Cover. Cook on low 10 to 12 hours or high 4 to 5 hours. Makes 6 to 8 servings.

AMERICA'S POT ROAST

1	teaspoon salt
3	to 4 pounds beef chuck roast, browned
4	medium potatoes, cut in quarters
3	carrots, sliced
2	stalks celery, sliced
1	medium onion, sliced
1/2	cup hot water

Salt roast. In large skillet with oil, brown roast over medium heat. In slow cooker, place vegetables. Add roast and water. Cover. Cook on low 10 to 12 hours. Makes 6 to 8 servings.

POT ROAST ON THE GO

    3 to 4 pounds beef chuck roast
    1 (10¾ ounce) can cream of mushroom soup
    1 (1 ounce) envelope dry onion soup mix
    ¼ cup water

In slow cooker, place roast. In medium bowl, combine mushroom soup, onion soup, and water. Mix well. Pour mixture over roast. Cover. Cook on low 8 to 10 hours. Makes 8 servings.

CHUCK ROAST

    3 to 4 pounds beef chuck roast
    2 tablespoons oil
    ⅓ cup creamy horseradish
    ½ cup water

In large skillet, brown roast in oil over medium heat. In slow cooker, place roast. Spread top of roast with horseradish. Add water. Cover. Cook on low 8 to 10 hours. Makes 6 to 8 servings.

OH SO DELICIOUS ROAST

3 to 4 pounds beef chuck roast
1 (6 ounce) jar sliced dill pickles, undrained
1 medium onion, chopped
1 teaspoon mustard seed
4 cloves garlic, minced
1 (14 ounce) can crushed tomatoes with Italian seasoning

In slow cooker, place roast. Pour pickles with juice over top of beef. Add onions, mustard seed, garlic, and tomatoes. Cover. Cook on low 8 to 10 hours. Shred beef. Pile beef onto toasted rolls or buns. Makes 6 to 8 servings.

ITALIAN BEEF ROAST

3 to 4 pounds beef rump roast
1 (14 ounce) can beef broth
2 cups mild giardiniera

In slow cooker, place roast. Add broth and giardiniera. Cover. Cook on low 8 to 10 hours. Shred beef. Serve with crusty rolls. Makes 8 servings.

MIX IT & GO ROAST

3	pounds beef roast
2	(⅞ ounce) envelopes brown gravy mix
1½	cups water

In slow cooker, place roast. In medium bowl, combine gravy mix and water. Mix well. Pour gravy mixture over roast. Cover. Cook on low 6 to 8 hours. If beef roast is frozen, increase cooking time to 8 to 10 hours. Makes 6 servings.

ITALIAN STYLE BEEF ROAST

- 3 to 4 pounds beef rump roast
- 1 cup water
- 1 ($7/8$ ounce) package Italian dressing mix
- 1 (1 ounce) package au jus gravy mix
- 2 teaspoons Italian seasoning

In slow cooker, place roast. In small bowl, combine water, dressing mix, gravy mix, and seasoning. Mix well. Pour mixture over roast. Cover. Cook on low 8 to 10 hours. Makes 8 to 10 servings.

BEEF CHUCK ROAST

- 2 medium green bell peppers, cut into strips
- 1/2 cup chopped onion
- 3 pounds beef chuck roast, browned
- 1 teaspoon salt
- 2 ($14 1/2$ ounce) cans stewed tomatoes

In slow cooker, add peppers and onion. Place roast on mixture. Sprinkle salt over roast. Pour tomatoes over top of roast. Cover. Cook on low 8 to 10 hours or high 4 to 6 hours. Makes 6 servings.

DELICIOUS CHUCK ROAST

1 teaspoon salt
2½ to 3 pounds beef chuck roast
1 cup flour
⅓ cup oil
2 tablespoons butter or margarine
2 (10¾ ounce) cans cream of mushroom soup
½ cup evaporated milk

Salt roast, dredge in flour. In large skillet with oil and butter, brown roast on both sides. Place in slow cooker. In medium bowl, combine soup and milk. Mix well. Pour mixture over roast. Cover. Cook on low 8 to 10 hours. Makes 6 to 8 servings.

HOME-STYLE ROAST

4 to 6 pounds potatoes, peeled, quartered
4 carrots, sliced
1 small onion, sliced
2 (14 ounce) cans stewed tomatoes
3 pounds beef chuck roast, browned
1 teaspoon salt

In slow cooker, place vegetables. Add stewed tomatoes. Mix well. Place roast on mixture. Sprinkle salt over roast. Cover. Cook on low 10 to 12 hours or high 4 to 5 hours. Makes 6 to 8 servings.

SOUTHWEST BEEF ROAST

1½   cups thick and chunky salsa
1   cup beer or water
1   (16 ounce) can tomato paste
2   tablespoons taco seasoning
3   pounds beef rump roast

In medium bowl, combine all ingredients except
roast. Mix well. Place roast in slow cooker. Pour
mixture over roast. Cover. Cook on low 8 to 10
hours or high 3 to 4 hours. Makes 6 to 8 servings.

BEYOND EASY BEEF ROAST

3   to 4 pounds beef roast
1   (24 ounce) jar yellow banana peppers,
    with juice
2   cloves garlic, minced

In slow cooker, place roast. Pour peppers over
roast. Sprinkle garlic on top. Cover. Cook on low
10 to 12 hours. Makes 6 to 8 servings.

SUNDAY SUPPER ROAST

2 pounds boneless beef roast
4 potatoes, peeled, quartered
3 carrots, peeled, cut into 1½-inch pieces
1 (14 ounce) can stewed tomatoes
1 (1 ounce) package dry onion soup mix

In slow cooker, place roast. Add potatoes and carrots. In small bowl, combine tomatoes and soup mix. Pour over roast. Cover. Cook on low 8 to 10 hours. Makes 4 to 6 servings.

ANYTIME ROAST

4 pounds beef chuck roast
4 potatoes, peeled, quartered
½ pound baby carrots
1 (16 ounce) jar beef gravy
1 (10¾ ounce) can tomato soup
1 (1 ounce) package stew seasoning mix

In slow cooker, place roast. Add potatoes and carrots. In small bowl, combine gravy, soup, and seasoning mix. Pour over roast. Cover. Cook on low 10 to 12 hours.

TERIYAKI ROAST

    3   pounds beef roast, browned on all sides
    1/4 cup sliced onion
    2   cups teriyaki baste and glaze sauce

Place roast in slow cooker. Sprinkle onion over roast. Pour sauce over roast and onion. Cover. Cook on low 8 to 10 hours. Makes 6 to 8 servings.

CRAZY CAJUN POT ROAST

    2   pounds beef roast
    1   tablespoon Cajun seasoning
    1   (9 ounce) package frozen corn
    1/2 cup chopped green bell pepper
    1/2 cup chopped onion
    1   (14 1/2 ounce) can diced tomatoes, undrained

Rub beef with Cajun seasoning and place in slow cooker. Top with corn, pepper, and onion. Pour tomatoes over vegetables and roast. Cover. Cook on low 6 to 8 hours. Makes 4 to 6 servings.

BBQ ROAST BEEF

3   pounds boneless beef roast
2   (12 ounce) bottles barbecue sauce
½   cup water
1   cup sliced onion

In slow cooker, place roast. In small bowl, combine remaining ingredients. Pour sauce over roast. Cover. Cook on low 8 to 10 hours. Makes 6 to 8 servings.

BLACK EYED PEA ROAST

1½   teaspoons garlic salt
1   teaspoon pepper
3   pounds beef roast
1   (14½ ounce) can black eyed peas, drained
1   (12 ounce) can sliced potatoes, drained
2   (3 ounce) packages gravy mix
1   cup water

Salt and pepper roast. In slow cooker, place roast. In large bowl, combine remaining ingredients. Mix well. Pour mixture over roast. Cover. Cook on low 8 to 10 hours. Makes 6 to 8 servings.

A ROBUST BEEF BRISKET

3 to 3½ pounds corned beef brisket, fat trimmed
¾ teaspoon crushed red pepper
1 cup reduced sodium chicken broth
1 tablespoon Worcestershire sauce

In slow cooker, place beef. Sprinkle red pepper over beef. In small bowl, combine broth and Worcestershire sauce. Pour over beef. Cover. Cook on low 8 to 10 hours. Makes 8 servings.

IRISH CORNED BEEF BRISKET

6   potatoes, peeled, halved
1   pound baby carrots
4   pounds corned beef brisket, fat trimmed
3   cloves garlic, minced
6   onions, quartered
1   medium head cabbage, cut into 6 wedges

In slow cooker, place potatoes and carrots. Add enough water to cover. Place meat over potatoes and carrots. Sprinkle with garlic. Top with onions. Cover. Cook on low 8 hours. Add cabbage. Cover. Cook an additional 2 hours. Makes 10 to 12 servings.

BEEF SHORT RIBS

4   pounds beef short ribs, cut into pieces
1   (10¾ ounce) can beef broth
½   cup prepared horseradish

In slow cooker, place ribs. Cover. Cook on high 1½ hours. Drain. In small bowl, combine broth and horseradish. Mix well. Pour mixture over ribs. Cover. Cook on low 8 to 10 hours. Makes 8 servings.

COOK & SLICE BRISKET

  4   to 5 pounds beef brisket
  1   (1½ ounce) bottle liquid smoke
¼   cup water
  2   cups barbecue sauce

In large bowl, place brisket. Pour liquid smoke over meat. Cover. Refrigerate over night. In slow cooker, place brisket. Add water. Cover. Cook on low 10 to 12 hours. Last two hours of cooking, pour barbecue sauce over brisket. Makes 8 to 10 servings.

SLOW COOKER SWISS STEAK

  1   medium green bell pepper, chopped
  2   stalks celery, chopped
  1   (14 ounce) can tomatoes
  1   (14½ ounce) can tomato sauce
  3   pounds round steak, browned

In slow cooker, combine all ingredients, except steak. Mix well. Place steak on mixture. Cover. Cook on low 8 to 10 hours. Makes 6 servings.

AFTER WORK SWISS STEAK

1½   cups sliced carrots
  4   medium potatoes, sliced
  1   (14½ ounce) can diced tomatoes with
      Italian herbs, undrained
  1   (12 ounce) jar beef gravy
  2   to 3 pounds round steak, browned, cut
      into serving-sized pieces

In slow cooker, combine all ingredients, except
steak. Mix well. Place steak on mixture. Cover.
Cook on low 8 to 10 hours. Makes 6 servings.

Better
Homes
and Gardens®

Test Kitchen

MUSHROOM AND ONION SAUCED ROUND STEAK

2 pounds boneless beef round steak, cut
  3/4 inch thick in serving-sized pieces
1 tablespoon cooking oil
2 medium onions, sliced
3 cups sliced fresh mushrooms
1 (12 ounce) jar beef gravy
1 (1.1 ounce) package dry mushroom gravy mix

Trim fat from steak. In large skillet, brown beef, half at a time, in hot oil. Drain. Place onions in slow cooker. Place steak pieces and mushrooms on onions. In small bowl, combine beef gravy and mushroom gravy mix. Pour over all. Cover. Cook on low 8 to 10 hours or high 4 to 5 hours. Makes 8 servings.

BRISKET MARINADE

3 to 4 pounds beef brisket
1 (16 ounce) bottle Italian dressing

In large bowl, place brisket. Pour dressing over meat. Cover. Refrigerate overnight. Wrap brisket in aluminum foil. Place in slow cooker. Cover. Cook on low 8 to 10 hours. Makes 8 to 10 servings.

CREAMY STYLE SWISS STEAK

3 pounds round steak, browned
2 (10¾ ounce) cans cream of mushroom soup
1 cup evaporated milk
¼ cup water

In slow cooker, place steak. In medium bowl, combine remaining ingredients. Mix well. Pour mixture over steak. Cover. Cook on low 8 to 10 hours. Makes 6 servings.

PEPPERS AND SWISS STEAK

4 pounds top sirloin steaks, cut in serving-sized pieces
2 (14½ ounce) cans diced tomatoes
2 green bell peppers, sliced into ½-inch strips
1 medium onion, chopped
1½ teaspoons salt
1 teaspoon pepper

In slow cooker, place steak. Add tomatoes, bell peppers, onion, salt, and pepper. Cover. Cook on low 8 to 10 hours. Makes 10 servings.

ROUND STEAK AND MUSHROOM GRAVY

3 pounds round steak, cut into
   serving-sized pieces
1 tablespoon butter
1 (10¾ ounce) can cream of mushroom soup
1 (1 ounce) package dry onion soup mix
1¼ cups water

In large skillet over medium high heat, brown
steak in butter. In slow cooker, combine all
ingredients. Mix well. Cover. Cook on low 4 to 6
hours. Makes 6 to 8 servings.

ITALIAN STYLE ROUND STEAK

2 pounds round steak, fat trimmed, cut
   into serving-sized pieces
2 (15½ ounce) jars spaghetti sauce
1 onion, sliced
1 (4½ ounce) jar sliced mushrooms, drained

In slow cooker, place steak. Pour sauce over steak.
Top with onion and mushrooms. Cover.
Cook on low 6 to 8 hours. Makes 6 servings.

MIX IT QUICK MEAT LOAF

2 pounds lean ground beef
2 eggs
1 package saltine crackers, crushed
1 small onion, chopped
2 cups salsa

Coat inside of slow cooker with nonstick cooking spray. In large bowl, combine beef, eggs, crackers, onion, and 1 cup salsa. Mix well. Shape mixture into loaf. Place in slow cooker. Top with remaining cup of salsa. Cover. Cook on low 6 to 8 hours. Makes 6 servings.

MEXI MEAT LOAF

2 pounds lean ground beef
2 cups crushed corn chips
1 cup grated cheddar cheese
2/3 cup salsa
4 tablespoons taco seasoning
2 eggs, beaten

Coat inside of slow cooker with nonstick cooking spray. In large bowl, combine all ingredients. Mix well. Shape mixture into a loaf. Place in slow cooker. Cover. Cook on low 6 to 8 hours. Makes 6 servings.

HEARTY MEAT LOAF

- 2 pounds lean ground beef
- 1/2 cup chopped green bell pepper
- 1/2 cup chopped onion
- 1 cup cracker crumbs
- 1 egg
- 1 (7/8 ounce) envelope brown gravy mix
- 1 cup milk

Coat inside slow cooker with nonstick cooking spray. In large bowl, combine all ingredients. Mix well. Shape mixture into loaf. Place in slow cooker. Cover. Cook on low 6 to 8 hours. Makes 6 servings.

LAZY DAY MEAT LOAF

- 2 pounds lean ground beef
- 1 cup crushed saltine crackers
- 1 egg
- 1/3 cup diced onion
- 1/3 cup diced celery
- 1/2 cup diced tomato
- 2 (10¾ ounce) cans cream of mushroom soup

Coat inside slow cooker with nonstick cooking spray. In large bowl, combine all ingredients, except soup. Mix well. Shape mixture into loaf. Place in slow cooker. Pour soup over loaf. Cover. Cook on low 6 to 8 hours. Makes 6 servings.

TEXAS MEAT LOAF

- 2 pounds lean ground beef
- 1/2 cup salsa
- 2 eggs
- 1 cup crushed bread crumbs
- 1 1/2 cups shredded Mexican blend cheese, divided

Coat inside slow cooker with nonstick cooking spray. In large bowl, combine all ingredients, except 1/2 cup cheese. Mix well. Shape mixture into loaf. Place in slow cooker. Cover. Cook on low 6 to 8 hours. Sprinkle cheese over top. Cover. Turn off slow cooker. Let sit 5 minutes. Makes 6 servings.

MEAT LOAF FOR DINNER

- 2 pounds lean ground beef
- 1/2 cup tomato soup
- 1 egg
- 2 tablespoons dry onion soup mix
- 1/2 cup dry bread crumbs

Coat inside slow cooker with nonstick cooking spray. In large bowl, combine all ingredients. Mix well. Shape mixture into loaf. Place in slow cooker. Cover. Cook on low 6 to 8 hours. Makes 6 servings.

JUST A MEAT LOAF

2 pounds lean ground beef
1/2 cup stuffing mix
1 small onion, chopped
2 eggs
2 (10¾ ounce) cans tomato soup
1/4 teaspoon salt

Coat inside slow cooker with nonstick cooking spray. In large bowl, combine all ingredients. Mix well. Shape mixture into loaf. Place in slow cooker. Cover. Cook on low 6 to 8 hours. Makes 6 servings.

MIX IT UP MEAT LOAF

2 pounds lean ground beef
1 (6 ounce) package stuffing mix
3 eggs
1 cup ketchup

Spray inside of slow cooker with nonstick cooking spray. In large bowl, combine beef, stuffing, and eggs. Mix well. Shape mixture into loaf. Place in slow cooker. Cover. Cook on low 6 to 8 hours or high 4 hours. Spread ketchup over meat loaf. Cover. Cook an additional 20 minutes.

MEAT LOAF

- 2 pounds lean ground beef
- 5 slices bread, cubed
- 2 eggs
- 1 (1 ounce) package dry onion soup mix
- ¾ cup water
- ⅓ cup ketchup

Spray slow cooker with nonstick cooking spray. In large bowl, combine all ingredients. Shape mixture into loaf. Place in slow cooker. Cover. Cook on low 6 to 8 hours or high 3 to 4 hours. Makes 6 servings.

SHREDDED BEEF SANDWICHES

- 2 pounds beef flank steak
- 1 small onion, sliced
- 1 cup sliced mushrooms
- 2 medium tomatoes, chopped
- 1 cup barbecue sauce
- 2 teaspoons Italian seasoning

In slow cooker, place steak. Top with remaining ingredients. Cover. Cook on high 5 hours or low 8 to 10 hours. Remove steak and shred. Return to slow cooker. Stir well. Serve on buns. Makes 6 to 8 servings.

FRENCH DIP SANDWICHES

- 4 pounds beef roast, fat trimmed
- 2 (10¾ ounce) cans French onion soup
- 1 (10½ ounce) can beef broth
- 6 French rolls, toasted
- 6 slices mozzarella cheese

In slow cooker, place roast. Add soup and broth. Cover. Cook on low 8 to 10 hours. Slice beef, place on rolls, and top with cheese. Makes 6 servings.

SANTA FE BEEF FAJITAS

- 2 pounds beef flank steak, sliced into ½-inch strips
- 2 (16 ounce) jars salsa
- 1 cup chopped onion
- 1 cup chopped green bell pepper

In slow cooker, combine all ingredients. Mix well. Cover. Cook on low 6 to 8 hours or high 3 to 4 hours. Serve with flour tortillas, grated cheddar cheese, sour cream, and guacamole. Makes 6 to 8 servings.

MEATBALL SANDWICHES

3 pounds frozen fully cooked meatballs
1 green bell pepper, chopped
1 onion, chopped
1 (15½ ounce) jar spaghetti sauce
6 French rolls
6 slices mozzarella cheese

In slow cooker, combine meatballs, pepper, onion, and spaghetti sauce. Mix well. Cover. Cook on low 4 to 5 hours. Spoon meatballs on rolls. Top with cheese. Makes 6 servings.

MEATBALLS AND GRAVY SANDWICHES

3 pounds frozen fully cooked meatballs
1 (10 ounce) jar beef gravy
1 (1 ounce) package dry onion soup mix
2 cloves garlic, minced
2 tablespoons water
6 French rolls
6 slices mozzarella

In slow cooker, place all ingredients, except rolls and cheese. Mix well. Cover. Cook on low 4 to 5 hours. Spoon meatballs on French rolls. Top with cheese. Serve with remaining sauce. Makes 6 servings.

TASTY BEEF BURGERS

1	(10¾ ounce) can gumbo soup
¼	cup ketchup
1	tablespoon mustard
1½	pounds lean ground beef, browned, drained
1	teaspoon salt

In slow cooker, combine all ingredients. Cover.
Cook on high 1 hour. Reduce heat to low. Cover.
Cook on low 1 hour. Makes 4 to 6 servings.

PIZZA SLOPPY JOES

2	pounds lean ground beef
1	cup chopped onion
2	(14 ounce) jars pizza sauce
1	(3½ ounce) package sliced pepperoni, chopped
½	cup chopped green bell pepper
8	sandwich buns
2	cups shredded mozzarella cheese

In large skillet over medium high heat, brown beef
and onion. Drain. In slow cooker, combine beef and
remaining ingredients, except for the buns and
cheese. Mix well. Cover. Cook on low 3 to 4 hours.
Makes 8 servings.

CORNED BEEF REUBENS

2 to 3 pounds corned beef brisket
2 cloves garlic, minced
10 peppercorns

In slow cooker, place corned beef. Top with garlic and peppercorns. Cover. Cook on low 8 to 10 hours. Slice beef thin. To make Reuben sandwiches, use pumpernickel bread, Swiss cheese, sauerkraut, and Thousand Island dressing along with the sliced beef. Makes 6 servings.

FLAVOR PACKED PORK ROAST

4 cups herb-seasoned stuffing cubes
3/4 cup chicken broth
1/2 cup chopped onion
2 to 2 1/2 pounds boneless pork loin roast
1/2 cup apricot jam
2 tablespoons vinegar

Coat inside slow cooker with nonstick cooking spray. In medium bowl, combine stuffing, broth, and onion. Place mixture in slow cooker. Place roast on top of mixture. In small bowl, combine jam and vinegar. Mix well. Brush mixture over roast. Cover. Cook on low 8 to 10 hours. Stir stuffing before serving. Makes 6 servings.

BONELESS PORK ROAST

3 to 4 pounds boneless pork roast
2 (14½ ounce) cans crushed tomatoes
2 tablespoons dry onion soup mix
⅓ cup sliced onion

In slow cooker, place roast. In medium bowl, combine remaining ingredients. Mix well. Pour mixture over roast. Cover. Cook on low 8 to 10 hours or high 4 to 5 hours. Makes 6 to 8 servings.

PORK ROAST & CHERRIES

2 to 3 pounds boneless pork roast
¼ cup pineapple juice
1 (20 ounce) can cherries

In slow cooker, place roast. Pour juice over roast. Cover. Cook on low 4 hours. Remove lid. Cover roast with cherries. Cover. Cook an additional 2 to 4 hours. Makes 6 servings.

GARLIC PORK ROAST

2½   pounds boneless pork loin roast
1   tablespoon chopped fresh thyme
½   teaspoon salt
2   tablespoons olive oil
2   cloves garlic, minced

In slow cooker, place roast. In small bowl, combine remaining ingredients. Mix well. Rub mixture over roast. Cover. Cook on low 6 to 8 hours. Makes 6 to 8 servings.

PORK LOIN ROAST

4   pounds boneless pork loin roast
1   cup apple jelly
2   tablespoons cider vinegar
1   cup ketchup

In slow cooker, place roast. In medium bowl, combine remaining ingredients. Mix well. Spoon mixture over roast. Cover. Cook on low 8 to 10 hours. Makes 6 to 8 servings.

ORANGE GLAZED PORK ROAST

- 3 to 4 pounds pork shoulder roast
- 1 (6 ounce) can frozen orange juice, thawed
- 1/4 cup brown sugar
- 1/2 teaspoon salt
- 1/4 teaspoon pepper
- 1/4 teaspoon allspice

In slow cooker, place roast. In small bowl, combine remaining ingredients. Pour mixture over roast. Cover. Cook on low 8 to 12 hours. Makes 6 to 8 servings.

PORK ROAST

- 2 tablespoons vegetable oil
- 4 pounds boneless pork roast
- 1 onion, sliced
- 3 cloves garlic, minced
- 1 (15 ounce) can chicken broth

In large skillet with oil, brown roast on all sides over medium heat. In slow cooker, place onion. Top with garlic. Place roast in slow cooker. Pour chicken broth over roast. Cover. Cook on low 10 to 12 hours or high 4 to 5 hours. Makes 8 servings.

CRANBERRY ROAST

2 pounds boneless pork loin roast
2 (15 ounce) cans whole berry cranberry
   sauce
2 tablespoons sugar

In slow cooker, place roast. In medium bowl,
combine cranberry sauce and sugar. Pour mixture
over roast. Cover. Cook on low 8 to 10 hours. Makes
4 to 6 servings.

KRAUT & CHOPS

- 3 pounds pork chops
- 1/2 teaspoon garlic powder
- 1/2 teaspoon pepper
- 1 (32 ounce) bag sauerkraut, rinsed
- 1 cup applesauce

In slow cooker, place chops. Sprinkle with garlic powder and pepper. Pour sauerkraut and then applesauce over chops. Cover. Cook on low 8 to 10 hours. Makes 6 to 8 servings.

PIZZA TASTING PORK CHOPS

- 6 pork chops, 1 inch thick, fat removed
- 2 tablespoons oil
- 2 cups pizza sauce
- 1/2 teaspoon dried basil leaves
- 1 small onion, chopped

In large skillet with oil, brown pork chops over medium heat. In slow cooker, place pork chops. In medium bowl, combine pizza sauce, dried basil, and onion. Mix well. Pour mixture over chops. Cover. Cook on low 8 to 10 hours. Makes 6 servings.

CELERY AROUND PORK CHOPS

6 pork chops, 1 inch thick, fat removed
1 (10¾ ounce) can cream of celery soup
¼ cup water
2 stalks celery, chopped

In slow cooker, place chops. In medium bowl, combine soup, water, and celery. Mix well. Pour over chops. Cover. Cook on low 8 to 10 hours. Makes 6 servings.

CRAN-APPLE PORK CHOPS

4 center-cut boneless pork loin chops, ¾ inch thick
5 McIntosh apples, peeled, cored, cut into chunks
½ cup dried cranberries
1 cup cranberry-apple juice

In slow cooker, place pork chops. Add remaining ingredients. Cover. Cook on low 6 to 8 hours. Makes 4 servings.

PORK CHOPS & SWEET POTATOES

1 cup chunky applesauce
3 large sweet potatoes, sliced
1 tablespoon brown sugar
6 boneless pork loin chops
1 (15 ounce) can whole berry cranberry sauce

In slow cooker, place applesauce. Layer sweet potatoes over applesauce. Sprinkle brown sugar over potatoes. Place chops over potatoes. Spoon cranberry sauce over chops. Cover. Cook on low 8 to 10 hours. Makes 6 servings.

NUTTY MAPLE CHOPS

6 boneless pork loin chops, 1 inch thick
1 teaspoon salt
6 tablespoons butter or margarine, melted, divided
3 tablespoons maple syrup
1/2 cup chopped pecans, toasted

Sprinkle chops with salt. Place 1 tablespoon butter in slow cooker. Place chops on butter. Cover. Cook on low 8 to 10 hours. In small bowl, combine remaining butter and syrup. Mix well. Remove chops to platter. Spread mixture over chops. Sprinkle with pecans. Makes 6 servings.

SWEET ORANGE PORK CHOPS

- 6 boneless pork loin chops
- 1 (12 ounce) jar orange marmalade
- 1/3 cup orange juice

In slow cooker, place chops. In medium bowl, combine remaining ingredients. Mix well. Pour mixture over chops. Cover. Cook on low 8 to 10 hours. Makes 6 servings.

SWEET & SOUR CHOPS

- 6 to 8 pork chops, 1/2 inch thick
- 2 cups sweet and sour sauce

Spoon sauce over each chop. Place in slow cooker. Cover. Cook on low 8 to 10 hours. Makes 6 to 8 servings.

ORIENTAL CHOPS

1 (16 ounce) package frozen oriental
   vegetables
6 pork chops
1 (12 ounce) bottle sweet and sour sauce
1/3 cup water
1 cup frozen pea pods

In slow cooker, add vegetables. Arrange chops on
top of vegetables. In medium bowl, combine sauce
and water. Mix well. Pour over chops. Cover. Cook
on low 8 to 10 hours. Turn to high and add pea
pods. Cover. Cook an additional 20 minutes. Makes
6 servings.

PORK CHOPS

6 boneless pork loin chops, 1 inch thick
1 tablespoon olive oil
1 onion, chopped
2 cups pasta sauce

In large skillet with oil, brown chops over medium
high heat. In slow cooker, place chops. Sprinkle
onion over chops. Pour sauce over chops and onion.
Cover. Cook on low 8 to 10 hours. Makes 6 servings.

SHORTCUT PORK CHOPS

1 medium onion, sliced
6 pork chops
2 (10¾ ounce) cans cream of celery soup
½ cup evaporated milk
½ teaspoon salt

In slow cooker, place onion. Arrange chops on onion. In medium bowl, combine remaining ingredients. Mix well. Pour mixture over chops. Cover. Cook on low 8 to 10 hours. Makes 6 servings.

TEXAS STYLE CHOPS

4 to 5 butterfly pork chops
2 (10¾ ounce) cans tomato soup
1 (7 ounce) can chopped green chiles
1 cup shredded Monterey Jack cheese

In slow cooker, place chops. Add soup and chiles. Cover. Cook on low 8 to 10 hours. Sprinkle cheese over mixture. Cover. Let set 10 minutes. Makes 4 to 5 servings.

SWISS PORK CHOPS

6 to 8 pork chops
2 (14½ ounce) cans chopped tomatoes
1 cup tomato sauce
1 cup chopped green bell pepper
½ cup chopped onion
1 teaspoon salt

In slow cooker, place chops. In large bowl, combine all remaining ingredients. Mix well. Pour mixture over chops. Cover. Cook on low 10 to 12 hours. Makes 6 to 8 servings.

TERIYAKI PORK

1 pound boneless pork shoulder, cut into 1-inch cubes
1 small onion, sliced
1 (5 ounce) can sliced bamboo shoots, drained
½ cup teriyaki baste and glaze
1 teaspoon gingerroot
1 (16 ounce) package frozen broccoli, carrots, and water chestnuts, thawed

In slow cooker, combine pork, onion, and bamboo shoots. In small bowl, combine teriyaki baste and gingerroot. Add to slow cooker. Mix well. Cover. Cook on low 6 to 7 hours. Add vegetables to slow cooker. Cover. Cook on high an additional 15 minutes. Serve over rice. Makes 5 servings.

IN A HURRY PORK CHOPS

  4 pork chops
  1 (16 ounce) bottle Italian dressing

In slow cooker, place pork chops. Pour dressing over chops. Cover. Cook on low 6 to 8 hours. Makes 4 servings.

GLAZED COVER PORK LOIN

  1 (16 ounce) package baby carrots
  4 boneless pork loin chops
  1 (8 ounce) jar apricot preserves

In slow cooker, place carrots. Top with pork. Brush pork with preserves. Cover. Cook on low 6 to 8 hours. Makes 4 servings.

PORK TENDERLOINS

2 pounds boneless pork loin
1 medium onion, sliced
2 apples, peeled, chopped
2 tablespoons apple jelly
1 tablespoon cider vinegar

In slow cooker, combine all ingredients. Cover.
Cook on low 8 to 10 hours. Serve over rice.
Makes 4 servings.

NUTS ABOUT PORK

1 tablespoon soy sauce
1 tablespoon oil
4 cloves garlic, minced
1/4 cup packed brown sugar
1 1/2 pounds lean pork strips
1/2 cup cashews

In small bowl, combine soy sauce, oil, garlic,
and brown sugar. Mix well. In slow cooker,
place pork. Top with mixture. Cover. Cook on low
5 to 6 hours or high 2 1/2 to 3 hours. Makes
4 to 6 servings.

SPOUT ABOUT BBQ PORK

- 2 to 3 pounds boneless pork loin
- 1 cup cola
- ¾ cup barbecue sauce
- ¼ cup ketchup

In slow cooker, place pork. In small bowl, combine cola, sauce, and ketchup. Mix well. Pour mixture over pork. Cover. Cook on low for 8 to 10 hours. Makes 6 to 8 servings.

SHREDDED PORK FOR TACOS

2 pounds boneless pork roast
1 (4 ounce) can chopped green chiles
1/2 teaspoon garlic salt
1/2 teaspoon pepper

In slow cooker, combine all ingredients. Cover.
Cook on low 8 to 10 hours or until meat is tender.
Use fork to shred pork. Makes 6 servings.

HONEY–MUSTARD BARBECUE PORK RIBS

3 1/2 pounds boneless pork country-style ribs
1 cup bottled barbecue sauce
1 (8 ounce) jar honey mustard
2 teaspoons zesty herb grill-seasoning blend

Place ribs in slow cooker. In a small bowl, stir
together barbecue sauce, honey mustard, and seasoning
blend. Pour over ribs in cooker. Stir to coat.
Cover. Cook on low 8 to 10 hours or on
high 4 to 5 hours. Transfer ribs to a
serving platter. Strain sauce; skim fat
from sauce. Drizzle some of the sauce
over the ribs and pass remaining sauce.

Better Homes and Gardens®
Test Kitchen

BARBECUE PORK RIBS

3	to 3½ pounds pork ribs, cut into serving-sized pieces
½	teaspoon salt
½	teaspoon pepper
1	large onion, sliced
2	(16 ounce) jars barbecue sauce
⅓	cup maple syrup
2	tablespoons packed brown sugar

Sprinkle ribs with salt and pepper. Place ribs on cookie sheet. Broil 15 minutes until brown. Drain. Combine remaining ingredients. Mix well. Arrange ribs over onions. Pour mixture over ribs. Cover. Cook on low 8 to 10 hours. Makes 6 servings.

CHOP STICK RIBS

½	cup sweet and sour sauce
¼	cup soy sauce
1	clove garlic, minced
3	to 4 pounds pork ribs

In small bowl, combine sweet and sour sauce, soy sauce, and garlic. Mix well. Brush sauce over ribs. In slow cooker, place ribs. Pour remaining ingredients over ribs. Cover. Cook on low 8 to 10 hours. Makes 6 to 8 servings.

COUNTRY BBQ RIBS

2½ to 3 pounds boneless country-style pork ribs
½ cup ketchup
½ cup honey
¼ cup soy sauce
2 cloves garlic, minced

In slow cooker, place ribs. In small bowl, combine remaining ingredients. Mix well. Pour mixture over ribs. Cover. Cook on low 8 to 10 hours. Makes 4 servings.

PORK BABY BACK RIBS

1 teaspoon salt
1 teaspoon dried thyme leaves
3 to 3½ pounds pork baby back ribs, cut into 4-rib-size portions
½ cup ketchup
3 tablespoons brown sugar
1 tablespoon Worcestershire sauce
1 tablespoon soy sauce

Rub salt and thyme over ribs. Place ribs in slow cooker. Cover. Cook on low 8 to 10 hours. Drain. In small bowl, combine remaining ingredients. Mix well. Pour over ribs. Cover. Cook on high an additional 30 to 40 minutes. Makes 6 servings.

EASY BARBECUE RIBS

$2\frac{1}{2}$ to 3 pounds spareribs
1 large onion, sliced
2 cups barbecue sauce

Place ribs on cookie sheet. Place under broiler for 15 minutes to brown. Drain. Slice ribs into serving pieces. Add onion to slow cooker. Place ribs on top of onions. Pour sauce over ribs. Cover. Cook on low 8 to 10 hours. Makes 4 to 6 servings.

BARBECUE SPARERIBS

3 to 4 pounds spareribs
1 large onion, sliced
1 (24 ounce) bottle barbecue sauce

In slow cooker, place spareribs. Top with onion. Pour barbecue sauce over onion. Cover. Cook on high $1\frac{1}{2}$ hours. Drain off fat. Turn to low and cook an additional 8 hours. Makes 4 to 6 servings.

FORK TENDER SHORT RIBS

4   pounds beef short ribs
1   medium onion, sliced
1   (12 ounce) jar beef gravy
1   (7/8 ounce) envelope beef gravy mix

In slow cooker, place ribs. Cover with onion. In a medium bowl, combine gravy and dry gravy mix. Pour over top. Cover. Cook on low 9 to 11 hours. Makes 6 servings.

PORK RIBS & KRAUT

2½   to 3 pounds country-style ribs
2   cups tomato juice
3   tablespoons honey
1   (28 ounce) can sauerkraut, rinsed, drained

In slow cooker, place ribs. In large bowl, combine remaining ingredients. Mix well. Pour mixture over ribs. Cover. Cook on low 8 to 10 hours or high 3 to 4 hours. Makes 6 servings.

TANGY RIBS

1	(8 ounce) bottle French salad dressing
1	onion, chopped
2	cloves garlic, minced
1½	to 2 pounds pork ribs

In small bowl, combine dressing, onion, and garlic. Mix well. Brush onto ribs. In slow cooker, place ribs. Pour remaining dressing mix over ribs. Cover. Cook on low 6 to 8 hours. Makes 4 to 6 servings.

ORANGE GLAZED HAM

5	pounds ham
1/3	cup orange marmalade
1	tablespoon Dijon mustard
1	large oven roasting bag

In roasting bag, place ham. In small bowl, combine orange marmalade and mustard. Mix well. Spread mixture over ham. Seal bag and poke 4 holes in top of bag to vent. Place bag in slow cooker. Cook on low 8 to 10 hours. Makes 8 servings.

HAM WITH COLA

1/2 cup packed brown sugar
1 teaspoon creamy horseradish
1 teaspoon dry mustard
1/3 cup cola
3 or 4 pounds precooked ham

In small bowl, combine brown sugar, horseradish, mustard, and soda. Mix well. In slow cooker, place ham. Brush mixture on top of ham. Cover. Cook on low 6 hours or high 2 to 3 hours. Makes 10 servings.

GOOD 'N TASTY HAM

2 (1 pound) ham slices, fully cooked
1/2 cup water
1/3 cup honey mustard

Cut each ham slice into 4 serving pieces. In slow cooker, combine water and honey mustard. Place ham in mixture. Cover. Cook on low 4 to 6 hours or high 2½ hours. Makes 8 servings.

MOUTHWATERING HAM

3	pounds smoked boneless ham, fully cooked
1½	cups fruit chutney
1	cup sliced onion
1	tablespoon balsamic vinegar

Place ham in slow cooker. In small bowl, combine remaining ingredients. Pour over ham. Cover. Cook on low 6 to 8 hours. Makes 8 servings.

HONEY MUSTARD HAM

3	pounds cooked ham
1/3	cup apple juice
1/4	cup packed brown sugar
1	tablespoon Dijon mustard
1	tablespoon honey

In slow cooker, place ham. Add apple juice. In small bowl, combine brown sugar, mustard, and honey. Spread over ham. Cover. Cook on low 6 to 8 hours. Makes 6 to 8 servings.

HONEY BAKED HAM

3	to 3½ pounds smoked ham
4	pineapple rings
¼	cup honey
2	tablespoons pineapple juice
¼	cup packed brown sugar

In slow cooker, place ham. Arrange pineapple rings on top. In small bowl, combine remaining ingredients. Mix well. Spoon mixture over ham. Cover. Cook on low 7 to 8 hours. Makes 6 servings.

PINEAPPLE OVER HAM

3½	to 4 pounds fully cooked ham
½	cup pineapple juice
1	cup crushed pineapple
⅓	cup packed brown sugar
1	teaspoon mustard

In slow cooker, place ham. In medium bowl, combine remaining ingredients. Mix well. Spread mixture over ham. Cover. Cook on low 8 to 10 hours. Makes 6 to 8 servings.

PEACH GLAZED HAM

4 to 5 pounds fully cooked ham
2/3 cup peach preserves
1/2 cup red raspberry jam

In slow cooker, place ham. Cover. Cook on low 3 to
4 hours. Spread preserves and jam over ham. Cover.
Cook an additional 4 to 5 hours. Makes 8 to 10
servings.

BBQ HAM SLICES

1½ pounds ham, cut into ½-inch slices
3/4 cup honey mustard barbecue sauce
1/2 cup orange marmalade

In slow cooker, place ham slices. In small bowl,
combine barbecue sauce and marmalade. Pour sauce
over ham. Cover. Cook on low 3 to 4 hours. Makes
6 servings.

ITALIAN SAUSAGE DINNER

1 large green bell pepper, sliced
1 small onion, sliced
3 cloves garlic, minced
1 (16 ounce) package hot or mild Italian
   sausage, cut into 6 links
2 cups spaghetti sauce
¼ cup red wine

In slow cooker, place bell pepper and onion. In
large bowl, combine garlic, sausage, spaghetti
sauce, and wine. Mix well. Pour mixture over
vegetables. Cover. Cook on low 6 to 8 hours or
high 3 to 4 hours. Serve over hot spaghetti.
Makes 6 servings.

CITY SLICKER BRATWURST

1   large onion, sliced
2   tablespoons vegetable oil
1½ pounds bratwurst
1   (12 ounce) can beer

In slow cooker, place onion. In large skillet
with oil, lightly brown bratwurst. Drain. Place
on onion. Pour beer over top. Cover. Cook on low
4 to 6 hours. Makes 4 to 6 servings.

TANGY BARBECUE BEEF

1	3-pound fresh beef brisket
2	tablespoons chili powder
1	teaspoons celery seeds
1/2	teaspoon salt
1/2	teaspoon ground black pepper
2	onions, thinly sliced
1	cup bottled smoke-flavor barbecue sauce
1/2	cup beer or ginger ale
8	large sandwich buns or Portuguese rolls, split and toasted (optional)
	Bottled hot pepper sauce
	Mango slices

Trim fat from brisket. Combine chili powder, celery seeds, salt, and pepper in a small bowl. Rub spice mixture onto all sides of the brisket. Place half of the onion slices in bottom of the slow cooker. Place brisket on the onions. Layer remaining onions on top of the brisket. Combine barbecue sauce and beer or gingerale; pour over brisket and onions. Cover; cook on low-heat for 10 to 12 hours. Transfer meat to a cutting board; let stand 15 minutes. Cut brisket in half. Shred meat using 2 forks to pull meat apart. Return meat to sauce in the slow cooker. Cook on high-heat setting until heated through. Spoon beef and onion mixture onto half of each bun or roll using a slotted spoon. Season to taste with bottled hot pepper sauce. Top with mango. Cover with remaining bun or roll halves. Makes 8 sandwiches.

Better Homes and Gardens
Test Kitchen

LEISURE DAY LAMB CHOPS

- 2 tablespoons oil
- 6 lamb chops
- 1/2 cup orange juice
- 3 tablespoons honey
- 2 tablespoons cornstarch

In large skillet with oil, brown chops over medium heat. Drain. In small bowl, combine juice, honey, and cornstarch. Mix well. Brush lamb chops with mixture. In slow cooker, place chops. Cover. Cook on low 10 to 12 hours. Makes 6 servings.

HONEY DIJON CHICKEN

- 1/2 cup honey
- 1/4 cup Dijon mustard
- 1/4 cup finely chopped onion
- 4 skinless, boneless chicken breasts

In medium bowl, combine all ingredients, except chicken. Mix well. Coat each breast with mixture. Place in slow cooker. Cover. Cook on low 6 to 8 hours. Makes 4 servings.

PINEAPPLE CHICKEN

4 to 6 skinless, boneless chicken breasts
1 (20 ounce) can pineapple chunks, undrained
1 small green bell pepper, sliced in strips
½ cup packed brown sugar

In slow cooker, place chicken. In medium bowl, combine remaining ingredients. Mix well. Pour mixture over chicken. Cover. Cook on low 6 to 8 hours. Makes 4 to 6 servings.

APRICOT GLAZED CHICKEN

4 large skinless, boneless chicken breasts
1 cup apricot preserves
2 tablespoons chili sauce
1 teaspoon Dijon mustard

In slow cooker, place chicken. In small bowl, combine remaining ingredients. Mix well. Spoon mixture over chicken. Cover. Cook on low 7 to 8 hours. Makes 4 servings.

HONEY MUSTARD CHICKEN

4   skinless, boneless chicken breasts
3/4   cup Dijon mustard
1/4   cup honey

In slow cooker, place chicken. In small bowl, combine mustard and honey. Pour over chicken. Cover. Cook on low 6 to 8 hours. Makes 4 servings.

CRANBERRY CHICKEN

2½ to 3 pounds chicken thighs and/or
    drumsticks, skinned
1   (16 ounce) can whole berry cranberry sauce
2   tablespoons dry onion soup mix
2   tablespoons quick-cooking tapioca
3   cups hot cooked rice

Place chicken pieces in slow cooker. In a small
bowl, stir together cranberry sauce, dry soup mix,
and tapioca. Pour over chicken pieces. Cover.
Cook on low 5 to 6 hours or high 2½ to 3 hours.
Serve chicken and sauce over hot cooked rice.
Makes 6 servings.

Better
Homes
and Gardens®

Test Kitchen

GLAZE OVER CHICKEN BREAST

4   large skinless, boneless chicken breasts
1/2 cup apricot preserves
1   tablespoon chili sauce
2   teaspoons Dijon mustard

In slow cooker, place chicken. In small bowl, combine apricot preserves, chili sauce, and mustard. Mix well. Pour mixture over chicken. Cover. Cook on low 6 to 8 hours or high 3 to 4 hours. Makes 4 servings.

BERRY-LICOUS CHICKEN

6   skinless, boneless chicken breasts
1   (15 ounce) can whole berry cranberry sauce
1   cup maple syrup
1/2 cup soy sauce

In slow cooker, place chicken. In small bowl, combine remaining ingredients. Pour over chicken. Cover. Cook on low 8 to 10 hours. Makes 6 servings.

CRANBERRY LOVER'S CHICKEN

6   skinless, boneless chicken breasts
1   (15 ounce) can whole berry cranberry sauce
1   cup French salad dressing
2   tablespoons dry onion soup mix

In slow cooker, place chicken. In medium bowl, combine remaining ingredients. Mix well. Pour mixture over chicken. Cover. Cook on low 10 to 12 hours. Makes 6 servings.

APRICOT CHICKEN

6   skinless, boneless chicken breasts
1/2   cup apricot preserves
1/3   cup Russian salad dressing
1/2   (1 ounce) package dry onion soup mix

In slow cooker, place chicken. In small bowl, combine remaining ingredients. Pour mixture over chicken. Cover. Cook on low 8 to 10 hours. Makes 6 servings.

MUSHROOM CHICKEN

4 skinless, boneless chicken breasts, cut
  into bite-sized pieces
2 (4½ ounce) cans sliced mushrooms
1 (10¾ ounce) can cream of mushroom soup

In slow cooker, place chicken. Sprinkle mushrooms over chicken. Top with soup. Cover. Cook on low 6 to 8 hours. Serve over rice or noodles. Makes 5 to 6 servings.

LEMON CHICKEN

3	to 4 pounds roasting chicken
3	tablespoons butter
	Juice of 1 lemon
2	teaspoons grated lemon peel
1/2	teaspoon salt

Clean and pat dry chicken with paper towels. Place in slow cooker. Rub butter over chicken. Pour lemon juice over chicken. Sprinkle lemon peel and salt over chicken. Cover. Cook on low 8 to 10 hours. Makes 6 to 8 servings.

LEMON OVER CHICKEN

4	skinless, boneless chicken breasts
1	lemon, halved
1	teaspoon lemon pepper
1	teaspoon paprika

In slow cooker, place chicken. Squeeze half of lemon over chicken. Sprinkle lemon pepper and paprika over chicken. Slice remaining lemon and arrange over chicken. Cover. Cook on low 6 to 8 hours. Makes 4 servings.

SWEET & SOUR CHICKEN

    4   skinless, boneless chicken breasts, cut
        into 1-inch cubes
  1/2   cup chopped green bell pepper
    1   cup pineapple chunks
    1   cup orange marmalade
    2   teaspoons soy sauce

In slow cooker, combine all ingredients. Mix well.
Cover. Cook on low 6 to 8 hours. Makes 4 servings.

SWEET & TASTY CHICKEN

1 1/2   cups baby carrots
    6   skinless, boneless chicken breasts
1 1/2   cups sweet and sour sauce
    1   (20 ounce) can pineapple chunks, drained
    1   (16 ounce) package frozen broccoli, bell
        pepper, and onion, thawed and drained

In slow cooker, place carrots. Top with chicken.
Cover. Cook on low 8 to 10 hours. Drain liquid
from slow cooker. Pour sweet and sour sauce over
chicken. Add pineapple and frozen vegetables.
Cook on high an additional 1 hour. Serve over rice.
Makes 6 servings.

TASTE OF THE ORIENT CHICKEN

6   skinless, boneless chicken breasts
1   (20 ounce) can pineapple chunks, with juice
1/4 cup brown sugar
2   teaspoons soy sauce

In slow cooker, place chicken. In small bowl, combine pineapple, brown sugar, and soy sauce. Pour over chicken. Cover. Cook on low 6 to 8 hours. Makes 6 servings.

CHICKEN IN MUSHROOM GRAVY

6   skinless, boneless chicken breasts
1/4 cup chicken broth
1   (10³/4 ounce) can cream of mushroom soup
1   (4¹/2 ounce) jar sliced mushrooms, drained

In slow cooker, place chicken. In medium bowl, combine remaining ingredients. Mix well. Pour mixture over chicken. Cover. Cook on low 6 to 8 hours or high 3 to 4 hours. Makes 6 servings.

ROASTED CHICKEN

  8   skinless, boneless chicken breasts
  1   tablespoon olive oil
1½ teaspoons parsley flakes
  1   teaspoon seasoned salt
  1   teaspoon garlic pepper

Brush both sides of chicken with oil. Sprinkle with parsley flakes, seasoned salt, and pepper. Place chicken in slow cooker. Cover. Cook on low 8 to 10 hours. Makes 8 servings.

SHOPPING DAY CHICKEN

  6   skinless, boneless chicken breasts
  1   (15 ounce) can tomato sauce
  1   (4½ ounce) jar sliced mushrooms, drained
⅓ cup water
½ teaspoon Italian seasoning

In slow cooker, place chicken. In medium bowl, combine remaining ingredients. Mix well. Pour mixture over chicken. Cover. Cook on low 8 to 9 hours or high 4 to 5 hours. Makes 6 servings.

BACKYARD BBQ CHICKEN

6   skinless, boneless chicken breasts
1   onion, sliced
1   (16 ounce) bottle barbecue sauce

In slow cooker, place chicken. Top with onion.
Pour barbecue sauce on top. Cover. Cook on low 8
to 10 hours. Makes 6 servings.

ALMOST BBQ CHICKEN

2   pounds skinless, boneless chicken pieces
1   (8 ounce) bottle French dressing
2   tablespoons Worcestershire sauce
2   tablespoons ketchup
2   tablespoons brown sugar
1/4 teaspoon garlic powder

In slow cooker, place chicken. In small bowl,
combine remaining ingredients. Pour over chicken.
Mix well. Cover. Cook on low 8 to 10 hours. Makes
4 to 6 servings.

BARBECUE CHICKEN BREASTS

4 skinless, boneless chicken breasts
2 cups barbecue sauce
1/4 cup ketchup
2 tablespoons maple syrup

In slow cooker, place chicken. In medium bowl, combine remaining ingredients. Mix well. Pour mixture over chicken. Cover. Cook on low 6 to 8 hours. Makes 4 servings.

SPUNKY BBQ CHICKEN

4 skinless, boneless chicken breasts
1 cup barbecue sauce
1/2 cup packed brown sugar
1/3 cup Grey Poupon® mustard

In slow cooker, place chicken. In small bowl, combine barbecue sauce, brown sugar, and mustard. Mix well. Pour mixture over chicken. Cover. Cook on high 2 1/2 to 3 hours or low 6 to 8 hours. Makes 4 servings.

NEW MEXICO STYLE CHICKEN

6 skinless chicken breasts
2 (10 ounce) cans Ro-tel® tomatoes
 and green chiles, undrained
4 green onions, sliced
½ teaspoon salt

In slow cooker, place chicken. In medium bowl, combine remaining ingredients. Mix well. Pour mixture over chicken. Cover. Cook on low 8 to 10 hours. Makes 6 servings.

SALSA CHICKEN

6 skinless, boneless chicken breasts
1 (16 ounce) jar salsa

In slow cooker, place chicken. Pour salsa over chicken. Cover. Cook on low 8 to 10 hours. Makes 6 servings.

NACHO CHICKEN

6 skinless, boneless chicken breasts
1 (14½ ounce) can Mexican-style stewed
  tomatoes, chopped
1 (10¾ ounce) can nacho cheese soup

In slow cooker, place chicken. In small bowl,
combine tomatoes and soup. Mix well. Pour over
chicken. Cover. Cook on low 8 to 10 hours. Makes
6 servings.

CHICKEN BURRITOS

4 skinless, boneless chicken breasts, diced
1 (16 ounce) jar chunky salsa
1 green bell pepper, diced
1 onion, diced
4 to 6 tortillas
1½ cups shredded cheddar cheese

In slow cooker, combine chicken, salsa, pepper,
and onion. Cover. Cook on low 6 to 8 hours. Spoon
mixture into center of tortillas. Top with cheese
and roll to close. Makes 4 to 6 servings.

CHICKEN CACCIATORE

2 (9 ounce) packages frozen cooked chicken breast strips
2 (28 ounce) jars tomato pasta sauce
2 cups sliced mushrooms
1 cup shredded fresh Parmesan cheese

In slow cooker, combine all ingredients, except cheese. Mix well. Cover. Cook on low 6 to 8 hours. Serve over hot linguine. Sprinkle cheese on top. Makes 6 servings.

MIXED UP CHICKEN

1 (2½ ounce) jar sliced dried beef, rinsed
4 skinless, boneless chicken breasts
½ pound bacon
2 (10¾ ounce) cans cream of mushroom soup
½ cup chicken broth

In slow cooker, place beef. Wrap chicken breast with bacon, place over beef. In small bowl, combine soup and broth. Mix well. Pour over chicken. Cover. Cook on low 6 to 8 hours. Makes 4 servings.

KEEP IT SIMPLE CHICKEN

- 4   large skinless, boneless chicken breasts
- 1/2 teaspoon salt
- 2   (10 3/4 ounce) cans cream of mushroom soup
- 1   (4 1/2 ounce) jar sliced mushrooms, drained
- 1/2 cup evaporated milk

In slow cooker, place chicken. Sprinkle salt over top of chicken. In medium bowl, combine remaining ingredients. Mix well. Pour mixture over chicken. Cover. Cook on low 6 to 8 hours. Makes 4 to 6 servings.

CHIPPED BEEF CHICKEN

- 1   (6 ounce) jar sliced dried beef, rinsed, chopped
- 1   (10 3/4 ounce) can cream of mushroom soup
- 1/2 pint sour cream
- 6   skinless, boneless chicken breasts

In small bowl, combine beef, soup, and sour cream. In slow cooker, place chicken. Pour beef mixture over chicken. Cover. Cook on low 8 to 10 hours. Makes 6 servings.

ITALIAN CHICKEN

- 6 skinless, boneless chicken breasts
- 1 green bell pepper, sliced
- 1 onion, sliced
- 1 (8 ounce) bottle Italian salad dressing

In slow cooker, place chicken. Top with pepper and onion. Pour dressing over top. Cover. Cook on low 8 to 10 hours. Makes 6 servings.

SIMPLY CHICKEN

- 5 skinless, boneless chicken breasts
- 2 tablespoons melted butter or margarine
- 1 teaspoon seasoned salt
- 1/2 teaspoon pepper

In slow cooker, place chicken. Drizzle butter over chicken. Sprinkle seasoned salt and pepper over chicken. Cover. Cook on low 8 to 9 hours. Makes 5 servings.

SWISS SLOW COOKED CHICKEN

- 8 skinless, boneless chicken breasts
- 8 slices Swiss cheese
- 2 (10¾ ounce) cans cream of mushroom soup
- ¼ cup chicken broth
- 1 cup herb-seasoned stuffing mix

In slow cooker, place chicken. Top with cheese slices. In medium bowl, combine soup and broth. Mix well. Pour mixture over chicken. Sprinkle stuffing on top. Cover. Cook on low 8 to 10 hours. Makes 8 servings.

GARLIC CHICKEN

- 4 skinless, boneless chicken breasts
- 1 tomato, chopped
- 1 (1 ounce) dry herb and garlic soup mix
- ⅓ cup water
- 1 tablespoon olive oil

In slow cooker, place chicken. Arrange tomato over chicken. In small bowl, combine soup mix, water, and olive oil. Pour over tomato and chicken. Cover. Cook on low 6 to 8 hours. Makes 4 servings.

CHICKEN CORDON BLUE

- 4 skinless, boneless chicken breasts, pounded thin
- 4 slices deli ham
- 4 slices Swiss cheese
- 1 (10¾ ounce) can cream of mushroom soup
- ¼ cup milk

On each chicken breast layer ham and cheese. Roll up, securing with a toothpick. In small bowl, combine soup and milk. Place chicken in slow cooker. Pour mixture over chicken. Cover. Cook on low 6 to 8 hours. Makes 4 servings.

PEPPER CHICKEN

- 8 skinless, boneless chicken breasts
- 2 green bell peppers, sliced
- 1 onion, sliced
- 2 cups pasta sauce

In slow cooker, place chicken. Top with peppers and onion. Pour sauce over ingredients. Cover. Cook on low 10 to 12 hours. Makes 8 servings.

CREAMY GARLIC CHICKEN

4 skinless, boneless chicken breast halves
1 (10¾ ounce) can cream of garlic soup
½ cup milk

In slow cooker, place chicken. In small bowl, combine soup and milk. Pour mixture over chicken. Cover. Cook on low 6 to 8 hours or high 3 to 4 hours. Makes 4 servings.

ANOTHER PEPPER CHICKEN

6 skinless, boneless chicken breasts
2 green bell peppers, sliced
1 (14 ounce) can stewed tomatoes
½ (6 ounce) bottle Italian salad dressing

In slow cooker, place chicken. Add green bell pepper. In small bowl, combine tomatoes and dressing. Pour mixture over peppers and chicken. Cover. Cook on low 8 to 10 hours. Makes 6 servings.

SWEET POTATO CHICKEN

3 sweet potatoes, peeled, cubed
1 onion, chopped
4 skinless, boneless chicken breasts
2 tablespoons butter, melted

In slow cooker, place sweet potatoes and onion. Place chicken on top of sweet potatoes and onion. Drizzle with butter. Cover. Cook on low 6 to 8 hours. Makes 4 servings.

HUNGRY MAN'S CHICKEN

- 6 potatoes, peeled, quartered
- 2 onions, sliced
- 6 skinless, boneless chicken breasts, halved
- 2 (10¾ ounce) cans cream of mushroom soup

In slow cooker, layer potatoes, onion, and chicken. Pour soup over top. Cover. Cook on low 8 to 10 hours or high 4 to 5 hours.

OLIVE CHICKEN

- 6 skinless, boneless chicken breasts
- ¼ teaspoon garlic salt
- 2 cups pasta sauce with green olives
- ½ cup grated Parmesan cheese

In slow cooker, place chicken. Sprinkle chicken with garlic salt. Pour sauce over chicken. Sprinkle cheese over sauce. Cover. Cook on low 8 to 10 hours. Makes 6 servings.

SAUCY CHICKEN SANDWICHES

- 4 skinless, boneless chicken breasts, cut into bite-sized pieces
- 1 (8 ounce) can tomato sauce
- 1/2 cup water
- 1 (1 1/4 ounce) package spaghetti sauce seasoning mix
- 1 (4 1/2 ounce) jar sliced mushrooms
- 6 to 8 buns
- 4 slices mozzarella cheese, cut in half

In slow cooker, combine chicken, tomato sauce, water, seasoning mix, and mushrooms. Cover. Cook on low 6 to 8 hours. Place chicken mixture on buns. Top with cheese and serve. Makes 6 to 8 servings.

CHICKEN LOAF

- 1 pound ground chicken
- 15 saltine crackers, crushed
- 4 green onions, finely chopped with tops
- 1 egg
- 1/3 teaspoon salt

Coat inside of slow cooker with nonstick cooking spray. In large bowl, combine all ingredients. Shape meat mixture into loaf. Place in slow cooker. Cover. Cook on low 3 to 4 hours. Makes 4 servings.

TASTY CHICKEN ITALIANO

    4   to 6 skinless, boneless chicken breasts
    1   (26 ounce) jar pasta sauce
    3/4 cup Italian seasoned dry bread crumbs
    2   cups shredded mozzarella cheese

In slow cooker, place chicken breasts. Pour pasta sauce over chicken. Sprinkle bread crumbs over sauce. Cover. Cook on high 3 to 4 hours or low 6 to 8 hours. Sprinkle cheese over mixture the last hour of cooking. Makes 4 to 6 servings.

STUFFING TOP CHICKEN

    6   skinless, boneless chicken breasts
    6   slices Swiss cheese
    1   (10 3/4 ounce) can cream of mushroom soup
    1/4 cup milk
    2   cups herb stuffing mix
    1/2 cup butter, melted

Spray slow cooker with nonstick cooking spray. Arrange chicken breasts in slow cooker. Top with cheese. In small bowl, combine soup and milk. Mix well. Spoon mixture over cheese. In small bowl, combine stuffing mix and butter. Sprinkle stuffing on top. Cover. Cook on low 8 to 10 hours or high 4 to 6 hours. Makes 6 servings.

FAMILY PLEASING CHICKEN

4	skinless, boneless chicken breasts
1/3	cup apple jelly
1	tablespoon honey
1	tablespoon Dijon mustard

In slow cooker, place chicken. In small bowl, combine jelly, honey, and mustard. Mix well. Brush mixture on chicken. Cover. Cook on high 1½ hours. Remove lid. Brush chicken with mixture. Cover. Reduce heat to low. Cook an additional 3 hours. Makes 4 servings.

EASY TO MAKE TURKEY

4½	to 5 pounds turkey breast
1	teaspoon poultry seasoning
2	(10¾ ounce) cans cream of mushroom soup
½	cup water

Rinse turkey and pat dry. Rub seasoning over turkey. In slow cooker, combine soup and water. Mix well. Place turkey on top of mixture. Cover. Cook on low 10 to 12 hours. Makes 8 servings.

TURKEY AND STUFFING

1	tablespoon butter or margarine
1/2	cup chopped onion
1	tablespoon apple jelly
1	(6 ounce) package stuffing mix
3/4	cup water
2	to 2 1/2 pounds skinless, boneless turkey breast half

In skillet over medium-high heat, sauté onion in butter until lightly browned. Add jelly and sauté until golden brown. In slow cooker, combine stuffing and water. Stir well. Place turkey breast on stuffing. Drizzle with onion mixture. Cover. Cook on low 6 to 8 hours. Makes 5 to 6 servings.

COMPLETE BBQ TURKEY MEAL

6	carrots, cut into 2-inch pieces
3	potatoes, cut into 2-inch pieces
2 1/2	to 3 pounds turkey, cut into bite-sized pieces
1	cup barbecue sauce
1/4	cup hot water

In slow cooker, layer carrots, potatoes, and turkey. In small bowl, combine barbecue sauce and water. Mix well. Pour sauce over turkey. Cover. Cook on low 8 to 10 hours. Makes 4 to 6 servings.

ROASTED TURKEY BREAST

3½   to 4 pounds skinless turkey breast
3   tablespoons butter or margarine
1   teaspoon salt
½   cup raspberry jam
1   teaspoon Dijon mustard

In slow cooker, place turkey. Rub with butter.
Sprinkle salt over top. Cover. Cook on low 10 to
12 hours. In small bowl, combine jam and mustard.
Mix well. Spoon mixture over turkey last hour of
cooking. Makes 6 to 8 servings.

TURKEY ANYTIME

4 to 6 pounds turkey breast
1 (15 ounce) can whole berry cranberry sauce
1/2 cup orange juice
1 (1 ounce) envelope dry onion soup mix

In slow cooker, place turkey. In medium bowl, combine cranberry sauce, orange juice, and onion soup mix. Mix well. Pour over turkey. Cover. Cook on low 8 to 12 hours. Makes 6 to 8 servings.

SEASONED TURKEY

2 pounds skinless, boneless turkey breast, cut into bite-sized pieces
1 onion, chopped
4 cloves garlic, minced
1/4 cup chicken broth
1/2 teaspoon crushed red pepper flakes
1 teaspoon salt

In slow cooker, combine all ingredients. Cover. Cook on low 6 to 8 hours. Makes 8 servings.

MEDITERRANEAN TURKEY

1½   pounds skinless, boneless turkey breast,
      cut into bite-sized pieces
¼   cup sliced black olives
¼   cup chopped onion
2   cloves garlic, minced
1   (14½ ounce) can stewed tomatoes

In slow cooker, combine all ingredients. Mix
well. Cover. Cook on low 6 to 8 hours. Makes
5 to 6 servings.

TASTY TURKEY

1   cup chicken broth
5   to 6 pounds turkey breast
4   tablespoons melted butter

In slow cooker, pour chicken broth. Add turkey.
Drizzle butter over turkey. Cover. Cook on low
10 to 12 hours. Makes 6 to 8 servings.

TURKEY AND VEGETABLES

4   carrots, cut into 2-inch pieces
3   potatoes, peeled, cut into wedges
2   celery stalks, cut into 1-inch pieces
1/2   cup chicken broth
3   pounds turkey breast
    Salt and pepper

In slow cooker, combine vegetables and broth. Place turkey on top. Salt and pepper to taste. Cover. Cook on low 10 to 12 hours. Makes 6 to 8 servings.

TURKEY LOAF

1   cup herb-seasoned stuffing mix, crushed
2   eggs
1   cup whole berry cranberry sauce, divided
2   pounds lean ground turkey

Coat inside slow cooker with nonstick cooking spray. In medium bowl, combine all ingredients. Mix well. In slow cooker, place meat mixture. Cover. Cook on low 4 to 6 hours. Heat remaining cranberry sauce in microwave for 1 minute. Serve sauce with loaf. Makes 4 servings.

FRESH COD FILLETS

- 2 large tomatoes, chopped
- 4 green onions, chopped
- 1 cup sliced fresh mushrooms
- 2 pounds fresh cod fillets
- 1/4 cup butter, melted
- 1 teaspoon salt

In slow cooker, combine tomatoes, onions, and mushrooms. Place cod on mixture. Drizzle butter and sprinkle salt over cod. Cover. Cook on low 2 1/2 to 3 hours. Makes 4 servings.

RED SNAPPER

- 2 medium green bell peppers, sliced
- 1 large onion, sliced
- 4 (8 ounce each) red snapper fillets
- 4 tablespoons butter
- 1 cup shredded Parmesan cheese

In slow cooker, layer green bell peppers and onion. Place red snapper over peppers and onion. Dot each snapper fillet with butter. Sprinkle with cheese. Cover. Cook on low 3 to 4 hours or until fish flakes. Makes 4 servings.

FLAVOR OF FLORIDA FISH

1½ pounds cod fillets
1 small onion, sliced
2 teaspoons grated orange peel
2 teaspoons grated lemon peel
2 tablespoons butter or margarine, melted

Spray slow cooker with butter-flavored nonstick cooking spray. In slow cooker, place fish. Add onion. Sprinkle with orange and lemon peel. Drizzle butter over all. Cover. Cook on low 1½ to 2 hours. Makes 5 to 6 servings.

CROCK THAT TUNA

3 pounds tuna, cut into serving-sized pieces
¾ cup prepared ranch salad dressing

Place tuna on heavy foil. Cover tuna with salad dressing. Seal foil and place in slow cooker. Cover. Cook on high 2 hours or low 4 to 6 hours. Makes 6 servings.

CLASSIC MARINARA SHRIMP

2 (15 ounce) jars refrigerated marinara sauce
3 cups frozen cooked shrimp without tails
1 cup sliced green onion

In slow cooker, combine all ingredients.
Mix well. Cover. Cook on low 2½ to 3 hours.
Makes 4 servings.

SWEET AND SOUR SHRIMP

1 (6 ounce) package Chinese pea pods,
   partially thawed
1 (13 ounce) can pineapple chunks, drained,
   juice reserved
1 (10 ounce) jar sweet and sour sauce
2 (4½ ounce) cans shrimp, rinsed, drained

In slow cooker, place pea pods and pineapple. In
small bowl, combine sweet and sour sauce and 3
tablespoons reserved pineapple juice. Mix well.
Add mixture to slow cooker. Mix well. Cover. Cook
on low 3 hours. Add shrimp. Mix well. Cover. Cook
an additional 15 minutes. Serve with rice. Makes
2 to 3 servings.

CAJUN SHRIMP AND RICE

1	(28 ounce) can tomatoes, cut up, undrained
1	(14 ounce) can chicken broth
1	cup chopped onion
1	cup chopped green pepper
1	(6 ounce) package long-grain and wild rice mix
1/4	cup water
2	cloves garlic, minced
1/2	teaspoon Cajun seasoning
1	pound cooked, shelled, deveined shrimp with tails
	Hot-pepper sauce (optional)

In slow cooker, combine tomatoes and juice, chicken broth, onion, green pepper, rice mix with seasoning packet, water, garlic, and Cajun seasoning. Cover. Cook on low 5 to 6 hours or high 3 to 3½ hours. If necessary, raise temperature to high. Stir shrimp into slow cooker. Cover. Cook an additional 15 minutes. If desired, serve with hot-pepper sauce.

Better Homes and Gardens®
Test Kitchen

Apple-Cherry Cobbler, page 278

Mocha Fondue, page 295

DESSERTS & FONDUES

APPLE-CHERRY COBBLER

1/2	cup sugar
4	teaspoons quick-cooking tapioca
1	teaspoon apple pie spice
1 1/2	pounds cooking apples, peeled, cored, and cut into 1/2-inch slices (4 1/2 cups)
1	(16 ounce) can pitted tart cherries
1/2	cup dried cherries
	Spiced Triangles (recipe below)
	Ice cream, such as butter pecan or cinnamon

Combine sugar, tapioca, and apple pie spice in
slow cooker. Stir in apple slices, undrained
canned cherries, and the dried cherries. Cover.
Cook on low 6 to 7 hours or high 3 to 3 1/2 hours.
Makes 6 to 8 servings.

SPICED TRIANGLES

In small bowl, combine 1 tablespoon sugar and
1/2 teaspoon apple pie spice. Unroll 1 package (8)
refrigerated crescent rolls. Separate triangles.
Brush 1 tablespoon melted butter over triangles;
lightly sprinkle with sugar-cinnamon mixture.
Cut each triangle into 3 smaller triangles.
Place on an ungreased baking sheet. Bake in a
375°F oven for 8 to 10 minutes or until bottoms
are light brown. Cool completely. Makes 24.

Better
Homes
and Gardens®

Test Kitchen

CHERRY DUMP DESSERT

2 (21 ounce) cans cherry pie filling
1 (18.25 ounce) box yellow cake mix
2/3 cup butter, melted

Coat inside slow cooker with nonstick cooking spray. In slow cooker, place pie filling. Sprinkle with cake mix. Drizzle butter over top. Cover. Cook on high 4 hours. Serve with ice cream.

JUST LIKE PEACH COBBLER

1/3 cup buttermilk baking mix
2/3 cup quick-cooking oats
1/2 cup packed brown sugar
1 teaspoon cinnamon
4 (canned or fresh) cups peaches
1/2 cup peach juice or water

Coat inside slow cooker with nonstick cooking spray. In medium bowl, combine buttermilk baking mix, oats, sugar, and cinnamon. Mix well. Place in slow cooker. Cover mixture with peaches and juice or water. Cover. Cook on low 5 hours. Remove lid. Cook an additional 20 minutes. Makes 6 servings.

PEACH TREE PEACHES

2 tablespoons butter or margarine, melted
6 fresh peaches, peeled, halved, pitted
1/2 cup packed brown sugar
1 teaspoon cinnamon
Whipped topping

In slow cooker, combine butter and peaches. Mix well. Sprinkle brown sugar over peaches. Cover. Cook on low 3 to 4 hours. Sprinkle cinnamon over peaches. Serve with whipped topping. Makes 4 servings.

PEACHES & CREAM

1/4 cup water
3 tablespoons butter or margarine, melted
6 fresh firm peaches, peeled, halved, pitted
1/4 cup packed brown sugar
1 tablespoon sugar
Ice cream

In slow cooker, pour water. Place peaches cut side up in water. Drizzle butter over top. In small bowl, combine brown sugar and sugar. Mix well. Sprinkle over peaches. Cover. Cook on low 3 to 4 hours or until tender. Serve with ice cream. Makes 6 servings.

HAWAII PINEAPPLE DESSERT

4 cups pineapple chunks
1 (11 ounce) can mandarin oranges, drained
1/3 cup packed brown sugar
1/4 cup rum
2 tablespoons butter or margarine
1/3 cup shredded coconut, toasted

In slow cooker, combine pineapple, oranges, brown sugar, rum, and butter. Mix well. Cover. Cook on high 1½ to 2 hours or until bubbly. Sprinkle coconut over mixture. Serve warm. Makes 6 servings.

GLAZED PINEAPPLE

4 (8 ounce) cans pineapple chunks
1¼ cups sugar
1/2 cup cider vinegar
1 teaspoon cinnamon
1/4 teaspoon ground cloves

Drain pineapple, reserving 1 cup juice. In slow cooker, place pineapple. In medium bowl, combine remaining ingredients. Mix well. Pour mixture over pineapple. Cover. Cook on low 2 to 3 hours.

CARAMEL APPLES

2 (14 ounce) packages caramels
1/4 cup water
8 medium apples

In slow cooker, combine caramels and water. Cover.
Cook on high 1 to 1½ hours, stirring frequently.
Insert sticks in stem of each apple. Dip apples in
mixture, coating entire surface. Place on greased
wax paper to cool. Makes 8 servings.

CARAMELS 'N APPLES

4 large cooking apples, cored
1/2 cup apple juice
1/4 cup packed brown sugar
2 tablespoons sugar
1/4 teaspoon cinnamon
8 caramel candies

In slow cooker, place apples. Pour juice on top.
In small bowl, combine brown sugar, sugar, and
cinnamon. Mix well. Sprinkle mixture over apples.
Put 2 caramels in core of each apple. Cover. Cook
on low 4 to 6 hours until apples are tender. Makes
4 servings.

STUFFED APPLES

 ½ cup water
 6 apples, cored
 ½ cup brown sugar
 2 tablespoons chopped walnuts
 2 tablespoons raisins
 1 teaspoon cinnamon
 2 tablespoons butter or margarine

In slow cooker, pour water. Place apples in water.
In small bowl, combine sugar, walnuts, raisins,
and cinnamon. Mix well. Fill core of each apple
with mixture. Dot each apple with butter. Cover.
Cook on low 6 to 8 hours. Makes 6 servings.

SLOW COOKED BAKED APPLES

 ½ cup water
 4 large cooking apples, cored
 ¼ cup sugar
 1 teaspoon cinnamon
 3 tablespoons raisins
 3 tablespoons butter
    Whipped cream

In slow cooker, pour water. In small bowl, combine
sugar, cinnamon, and raisins. Mix well. Fill each
apple core with mixture. Place apples in water.
Dot with butter. Cover. Cook on low 4 to 6 hours.
Serve hot with whipped cream. Makes 4 servings.

A LITTLE CHUNKY APPLESAUCE

- 8 large apples, peeled, cored, cubed
- 2/3 cup sugar
- 1/2 cup water
- 1 teaspoon cinnamon

In slow cooker, combine all ingredients. Cover. Cook on low 8 to 10 hours or high 3 to 4 hours.

APPLE AND CRANBERRY FRUIT DESSERT

- 8 apples, peeled, cored, sliced
- 1 1/2 cups fresh cranberries
- 1 cup boiling water
- 2 cups sugar, divided
- 1/4 cup cornstarch

In slow cooker, combine apples, cranberries, water, and 1 cup sugar. Cover. Cook on low 6 to 8 hours. In small bowl, combine remaining sugar and cornstarch. Add to slow cooker. Mix well. Cover. Cook an additional 20 minutes. Makes 6 servings.

ALMOST APPLE CRISP

- 3/4 cup packed brown sugar
- 2/3 cup quick-cooking oats
- 1/3 cup sugar
- 2 tablespoons flour
- 1/4 teaspoon cinnamon
- 5 cups peeled, sliced apples
- 1/3 cup raisins
- 3 tablespoons melted butter or margarine

In large bowl, combine brown sugar, oats, sugar, flour, and cinnamon. Mix well. Add apple slices and raisins. In slow cooker, place apple-oats mixture. Drizzle butter over mixture. Cover. Cook on low 6 to 8 hours.

CARAMEL ROLLS FOR DESSERT

- 1/4 cup butter or margarine, melted
- 1/2 cup brown sugar
- 1 teaspoon cinnamon
- 1/4 cup chopped walnuts
- 2 (8 ounce) packages refrigerated biscuits

Place butter in small bowl. In another small bowl, combine brown sugar and cinnamon. Mix well. Place nuts in another small bowl. Dip each biscuit in butter. Roll in brown sugar, then nuts. Place biscuits in slow cooker. Sprinkle remaining butter, brown sugar mixture, and nuts over top of biscuits. Cover. Cook on high 3 to 4 hours.

RAISIN BREAD PUDDING

- 6 cups dry French bread cubes
- 2/3 cup raisins
- 8 eggs
- 4 cups milk
- 2/3 cup sugar
- 1 teaspoon vanilla
- 1 teaspoon cinnamon

Spray inside of slow cooker with butter-flavored nonstick cooking spray. Place bread cubes in slow cooker. Top bread with raisins. In large bowl, combine eggs, milk, sugar, vanilla, and cinnamon. Mix well. Pour over bread cubes and raisins. Cover. Cook on high 3 hours.

RICE PUDDING

- 6 cups whole milk
- 1 cup regular white rice, uncooked
- 3/4 cup sugar
- 1 teaspoon cinnamon
- 1 teaspoon vanilla

In slow cooker, combine all ingredients. Mix well. Cover. Cook on high 2 to 3 hours. Stir twice during cooking.

FRUITY RICE PUDDING

- 2 (5½ ounce) packages rice pudding mix with raisins and spice
- 3 cups whole milk
- ½ cup snipped dried apricots or snipped dried cherries
- 2 tablespoons butter, softened
- ⅓ cup pecans or almonds, toasted

Lightly coat inside slow cooker with nonstick cooking spray. Combine the rice and spice packets from rice mixes, milk, and apricots in the slow cooker. Stir in butter. Cover. Cook on low 2 hours or until rice is tender. Turn off cooker or, if possible, remove crock from the slow cooker. Stir rice mixture. Let stand, uncovered, about 30 minutes to slightly cool before serving. To serve, stir well and spoon into individual dessert bowls. Top with toasted nuts. Makes 8 servings.

Better Homes and Gardens®

Test Kitchen

COOK DON'T BAKE BROWNIES

- 2 (14 ounce) cans sweetened condensed milk
- 4 (1 ounce) squares unsweetened chocolate, chopped
- 1 1/2 teaspoons vanilla
- 4 cups chocolate cookie crumbs
- 1/2 cup chopped walnuts

Coat inside slow cooker with nonstick cooking spray. Add milk and chocolate squares. Cover. Cook on high 1 to 1 1/2 hours or until chocolate has melted. Add vanilla and cookie crumbs. Mix well. Spread mixture in greased 13x9-inch baking pan. Sprinkle nuts over mixture. Press nuts down with a spoon. Cover. Chill. Makes 24 brownies.

PACK-N-GO COOKIES

- 1/3 cup cocoa
- 1/4 cup sugar
- 2 cups miniature marshmallows
- 1 cup peanut butter chips
- 1/2 cup butter
- 1 1/4 cups quick-cooking oats

In slow cooker, combine cocoa and sugar. Add marshmallows, peanut butter chips, and butter. Cover. Cook on high 1 1/2 hours. Reduce heat to low, stirring often, until mixture is smooth. Add oats. Mix well. Drop by heaping teaspoon onto wax paper. If mixture is too soft, let stand a few minutes before you drop mixture. Chill. Makes 24 cookies.

BUTTERSCOTCH KRISPIES

2 (6 ounce) packages butterscotch chips
1 tablespoon butter or margarine
6 cups Rice Krispies®

In slow cooker, combine butterscotch chips and butter. Cover. Cook on high 1 hour. Mix well. Cook on low until mixture has melted. Stir in Rice Krispies. Drop by tablespoon onto wax paper. Makes 2 dozen.

QUICK VANILLA FUDGE

2 cups vanilla chocolate chips
1 cup sweetened condensed milk
2 cups chopped almonds, toasted
1/2 teaspoon vanilla extract

In slow cooker, combine chips and milk. Mix well. Cover. Cook on high 1 hour. Mix well. Cook on low until mixture is hot and smooth. Add almonds and vanilla. Mix well. Spread in greased baking pan. Cover. Chill until firm. Cut into squares. Makes 2 dozen.

SWEET TREAT FUDGE

3 cups semisweet chocolate chips
1 (14 ounce) can sweetened condensed milk
1 cup chopped nuts
1½ teaspoons vanilla

In slow cooker, combine chocolate chips and milk. Cover. Cook on low 2 hours. Add nuts and vanilla. Mix well. Spread mixture into greased 9-inch-square pan. Chill until firm. Cut into squares. Makes 2 pounds.

CHOCOLATE CLUSTERS

2 cups semisweet chocolate chips
1 (4 ounce) package sweet chocolate
2 pounds white chocolate, chopped
1½ cups peanuts

In slow cooker, combine all ingredients, except peanuts. Cook on high 1 hour. Mix well. Cook on low until chocolate has melted. Add peanuts. Mix well. Drop by heaping teaspoon onto wax paper. Makes 3 dozen.

JAZZ UP CLUSTERS

1 2/3 cups peanut butter chips
2 tablespoons shortening
1 1/2 cups crushed thin pretzel sticks
1 cup honey graham cereal
1/2 cup sliced almonds

In slow cooker, combine peanut butter chips and shortening. Mix well. Cook on high 1 1/2 hours or until mixture has melted. Add pretzel sticks, cereal, and almonds. Drop mixture by heaping tablespoon onto wax paper. Cool. Makes 15 clusters.

CRAVING FOR CLUSTERS

4 cups peanut butter
2 (16 ounce) packages semisweet chocolate chips
2 (12 ounce) packages salted peanuts

In slow cooker, combine peanut butter and chocolate chips. Cover. Cook on low 2 hours or until mixture has melted. Add peanuts. Mix well. Drop mixture by heaping teaspoon onto wax paper. Cool. Makes 3 1/2 dozen.

CANDIED PRETZEL TREATS

2 (16 ounce) packages almond bark
4 tablespoons vegetable oil
4 dozen pretzels
1 cup confectioner's sugar

In slow cooker, combine almond bark and oil. Cook on high 1½ hours until melted. Mix well. Dip pretzels in mixture. Roll in sugar. Place on wax paper and chill until firm. Makes 48 pretzels.

NO FUSS CHOCOLATE DROPS

4 cups milk chocolate chips
2 teaspoons shortening
1 cup raisins
1 cup walnuts

In slow cooker, combine chocolate chips and shortening. Cover. Cook on high 1 hour. Reduce heat to low. Cook until mixture has melted. Add raisins and walnuts. Mix well. Drop mixture by heaping tablespoon on wax paper. Chill until firm. Makes 3½ dozen.

CHOCOLATE COVERED PEANUTS

2   pounds chocolate flavored almond bark
1   (12 ounce) package semisweet chocolate chips
3½ cups dry-roasted peanuts

In slow cooker, combine almond bark and chocolate chips. Cover. Cook on low, stirring every 15 minutes for 1½ hours. Add peanuts. Cook an additional 15 minutes. Drop by heaping tablespoon onto wax paper. Cool.

MILK CHOCOLATE FONDUE

1   (16 ounce) can chocolate-flavored syrup
1   (14 ounce) can sweetened condensed milk
1½ teaspoons vanilla extract

In slow cooker, combine chocolate and milk. Mix well. Cover. Cook on low 1½ hours. Add vanilla just before serving. Mix well. Serve with marshmallows, pound cake, angel food cake, or fresh fruit chunks.

FUDGY PEANUT BUTTER FONDUE

- 1/3 cup unsweetened cocoa powder
- 1/2 cup sugar
- 1/2 cup sweetened condensed milk
- 3 tablespoons peanut butter
- 1 teaspoon vanilla

In slow cooker, combine cocoa powder, sugar, milk, and peanut butter. Mix well. Cover. Cook on low 1 1/2 hours. Add vanilla just before serving. Mix well. Serve with fruit chunks or cake.

PEANUT BUTTER FONDUE

- 1 1/3 cups peanut butter
- 1 1/3 cups sweetened condensed milk
- 1 cup honey
- 1 teaspoon cinnamon

In slow cooker, combine all ingredients. Cover. Cook on low 1 1/2 hours. Stir after 30 minutes. Serve with sliced fruit or French bread chunks.

MOCHA FONDUE

½	pound milk chocolate, broken into pieces
1	cup sweetened condensed milk
¼	cup water
3	teaspoons instant coffee
½	teaspoon vanilla

In slow cooker, combine chocolate, condensed milk, and water. Cover. Cook on low 1 hour. Stir after 30 minutes. Add coffee and vanilla. Mix well. Cover. Cook an additional 30 minutes. Serve with pound or angel food cake and fruit slices.

CANDY BAR FONDUE

16	(1 ounce) chocolate candy bars, broken into pieces
30	large marshmallows
⅓	cup sweetened condensed milk
½	pint whipping cream

Spray inside slow cooker with nonstick cooking spray. Add candy bars, marshmallows, and condensed milk. Cover. Cook on low 1 hour. Stir every 30 minutes. Add whipping cream slowly. Mix well. Cover. Cook an additional 1½ to 2 hours. Serve with pound or angel food cake and sliced fruit.

CARAMEL FONDUE

- 1   (12 ounce) can sweetened condensed milk
- 1   cup brown sugar
- 1/2   cup light corn syrup
- 1/2   cup butter

In slow cooker, combine all ingredients. Mix well. Cover. Cook on low 2 to 3 hours. Serve with fruit slices and cookies. Makes 3 cups.

PEACHES AND CREAM FONDUE

- 2   (16 ounce) cans sliced peaches, drained
- 1 1/4   cups sweetened condensed milk
- 2   tablespoons confectioner's sugar

In blender, puree peaches. In slow cooker, combine all ingredients. Cover. Cook on low 1 1/2 hours. Serve with pound or angel food cake.

ADAPT MOST RECIPES TO A SLOW COOKER FOR HASSLE-FREE COOKING

CROCK POT AND SLOW COOKERS ARE THE SAME

You can prepare just about any type of meal in a Slow Cooker. There is nothing easier than putting ingredients into a Slow Cooker in the morning, and coming home to a hot cooked meal. Here are some tips to help adapt your recipes for successful cooking in your Slow Cooker. Several factors can affect your recipes, so **REMEMBER THESE TIPS.**

Tip 1 Cooking time in all recipes are approximations, affected by how much food is in the cooker, humidity, and the temperature of the ingredients when you add them. So note that cooking times in the recipes are ranges only.

Tip 2 To make cleanup easier, spray the inside of the Slow Cooker with nonstick cooking spray before adding food.

Tip 3 Meats will not brown in a Slow Cooker. If a recipes calls for meat to be browned, brown it in a skillet. The recipe will be better because it will enhance the flavor and decrease fat.

Tip 4 A Slow Cooker is great for tougher cuts of meat.

Tip 5 It is always better to thaw meat before placing it in the Slow Cooker. It will cook faster.

Tip 6 Fill cooker between half and two-thirds full.

Tip 7 Add vegetables to cooker first, then add meat. Vegetables cook slower than meat.

Tip 8 Cut vegetables in smaller pieces to ensure proper cooking.

Tip 9 Do not add as much water as regular recipes indicate. Use about half the recommended amount, unless it calls for rice or pasta. Liquids don't boil away as in conventional cooking.

Tip 10 If recipe calls for raw rice, add ¼ cup extra liquid per ¼ cup of raw rice.

Tip 11 If recipe calls for pasta or rice, cook until slightly tender.

Tip 12 If recipe calls for dry beans, it is best to cook beans before adding to recipe.

Tip 13 In the last hour of cooking it is better to add milk, sour cream, or cream to the recipe. Dairy products tend to curdle over long cooking periods. Condensed cream of soup or evaporated milk can be substituted in some recipes.

Tip 14 Processed cheeses tend to work better in Slow Cookers than natural cheese.

Tip 15 Juices can be thickened by adding corn starch during the last hour of cooking. Turn heat to high.

Tip 16 It is best to add ground seasoning near the end of cooking.

COOKING GUIDE FOR ADAPTING RECIPES

TIME GUIDE

If recipe says cook or bake	Slow Cooker on Low	Slow Cooker on High
15 to 30 minutes	4 to 6 hours	1½ to 2 hours
35 to 45 minutes	6 to 10 hours	3 to 4 hours
50 minutes to 3 hours	8 to 15 hours	4 to 6 hours

SLOW COOKER DON'Ts

• DON'T remove the lid during cooking unless a recipe calls for it. Every time you lift the lid, you slow the cooking time by 20 to 30 minutes.
• DON'T leave food in the slow cooker. Remove food within one hour.
• DON'T reheat food in a slow cooker because it takes too much time for food to reach a safe temperature.
• DON'T add water to clean the cooker until it has cooled.
• DON'T use metal utensils; use rubber, plastic, or wood to avoid damaging interior of the slow cooker.

EMERGENCY SUBSTITUTIONS

IF YOU DON'T HAVE:	SUBSTITUTE:
1 teaspoon allspice	½ teaspoon cinnamon and ½ teaspoon ground cloves
1 teaspoon baking powder	¼ teaspoon baking soda and 1 teaspoon cream of tartar
1 cup broth (beef or chicken)	1 bouillon cube dissolved in 1 cup boiling water
1 cup ketchup	1 cup tomato sauce, ½ cup sugar, and 2 teaspoons vinegar
2 teaspoons chives, finely chopped	2 teaspoons finely chopped green onion tips
1 tablespoon cornstarch	2 tablespoons all-purpose flour or 4 to 6 teaspoons quick-cooking tapioca
¾ cup cracker crumbs	1 cup bread crumbs
1 cup cream cheese	1 cup cottage cheese beaten until smooth
1 teaspoon dry mustard	1 tablespoon prepared mustard

IF YOU DON'T HAVE:	SUBSTITUTE:
1 cup sifted cake flour	1 cup minus 2 teaspoons all-purpose flour
1 cup self-rising flour	1 cup minus 2 teaspoons all-purpose flour plus 1½ teaspoons baking powder and ½ teaspoon salt
1 tablespoon fresh herbs	1 teaspoon dried herbs
1 cup sour milk	1 tablespoon lemon juice and enough milk to make 1 cup
1 cup buttermilk	1 cup plain yogurt
1 cup whole milk	½ cup evaporated milk
1 small fresh onion	1 tablespoon minced onion, dehydrated
½ cup brown sugar	2 tablespoons molasses in ½ cup granulated sugar
1 cup confectioner's sugar	1 cup granulated sugar plus 1 teaspoon cornstarch
½ cup maple sugar	1 cup maple syrup
2 cups fresh tomatoes	1 (16-ounce) can diced tomatoes
1 (15-ounce) can tomato sauce	1 (6-ounce) can tomato paste plus cup water
1 cup wine	13 tablespoons water, 3 tablespoons lemon juice, and 1 tablespoon sugar
1 teaspoon Worcestershire sauce	1 teaspoon bottled steak sauce
1 cup yogurt	1 cup sour cream

HERBS AND SPICES ARE USED FOR WHAT?

BASIL — Good with stews, roast beef, ground beef, lamb, fish, vegetables, and omelets.

BAY LEAVES — Has a pungent flavor. Good in seafood, stews, and vegetable dishes.

CARAWAY — Use in breads, soups, cakes, cheese, and sauerkraut.

CHIVES — Good in salads, fish, soups, and potatoes.

CILANTRO — Southwestern dishes, rice, beans, salads, fish, and chicken.

CURRY POWDER — A combination of spices that give a distinct flavor to meat, poultry, fish, and vegetables.

DILL — Both seeds and leaves may be used. Leaves can be used as a garnish or cooked with soup, fish, potatoes, and beans.

FENNEL — Has a hot, sweet flavor. Small quantities are used in pies and baked goods, and the leaves can be boiled with fish.

GINGER — It is a pungent root and is used in pickles, cakes,

HERBS AND SPICES ARE USED FOR WHAT?

cookies, preserves, soups, and meat dishes.

MARJORAM — It adds flavor to stew, stuffing, lamb, fish, poultry, and omelets.

MINT — It is great in beverages, soup, peas, carrots, lamb, cheese, preserves, and fruit desserts.

OREGANO — It can be used whole or ground, in pizza, tomato juice, fish, eggs, omelets, stew, gravy, poultry, and vegetables.

PAPRIKA — A bright red pepper that is used as a garnish for potatoes, salads, and eggs, and as a spice used in meat, vegetables, and soup.

PARSLEY — Can be used dried as seasoning or garnish. Use in fish, soup, meat, stuffing, and mixed greens.

ROSEMARY — It can be used to season fish, stuffing, beef, lamb, poultry, onions, eggs, bread, and potatoes. It is great in dressings.

SAFFRON — It is used in breads, soup, rice, and chicken.

SAGE — May be used in stuffing, fish, omelets, poultry, tomato juice, breads, and cheese spreads.

TARRAGON — Used in salads, sauces, fish, poultry, tomatoes, eggs, carrots, green beans, and dressing.

THYME — Leaves may be sprinkled on fish or poultry before baking or broiling.

IT MAKES HOW MUCH?

FOOD FOR INGREDIENTS	QUANTITY	YIELDS
Apple	1 medium	1 cup
Bread Crumbs	1 slice	¼ cup
Butter	1 stick	½ cup
Egg whites	8 to 10	1 cup
Egg yolks	10 to 12	1 cup
Lemon	1 medium	3 tablespoons lemon juice
Noodles, uncooked	1½ cups	2 to 3 cups cooked
Macaroni, uncooked	1¼ cups	2½ cups cooked
Spaghetti	8 ounces	4½ cups cooked
Nuts, chopped	¼ pound	1 cup
Nuts, walnuts, unshelled	1 pound	1½ cups
Onion, chopped	1 medium	½ cup
Rice, regular	1 cup	3 cups cooked
Rice, wild	1 cup	4 cups cooked
Sugar, brown	1 pound	2½ cups
Sugar, white	1 pound	2 cups

CHILI (See also: Soups and Stews)

CHOCOLATE

DESSERTS

POTATOES